Simple Bicycle Repair and Maintenance

Books by Ross R. Olney

Simple Gasoline Engine Repair

Simple Bicycle Repair and Maintenance

Simple Bicycle Repair and Maintenance

By ROSS R. OLNEY

DOUBLEDAY & COMPANY, INC.
GARDEN CITY, NEW YORK
1973

ISBN: 0-385-06199-4
Library of Congress Catalog Card Number 72-76234

Printed in the United States of America
First Edition

Acknowledgments

The author would like to thank the following for advice, photos, and technical information.
The Huffman Company, builders of "Huffy" Bicycles; Royce-Union, builders of the "Regent" bicycle; United Savings Helms Athletic Foundation; and especially Mr. Peter Kaszonyi of the Schwinn Bicycle Company for his generosity with technical information and assistance.

Contents

1

The Bicycle

If the Comte de Sivrac could know, he would probably be astounded at what happened to his toy. For when Norman Lezin, a bit more recently, offered to help his employees obtain bicycles if they would promise to ride them, he was overwhelmed at the results.

Lezin? De Sivrac?

De Sivrac was the man who conceived the grandfather of all bicycles, a rough wooden bar supported on two wheels, with a padded saddle, and which you pushed along with your feet. This 1790s invention didn't even have a steering apparatus. It was uncomfortable, inconvenient, and inefficient . . . . and comical-looking besides.

Yet when bike enthusiast Lezin, with a sad look at the exhaust fumes in the air and the crowded parking lot of his company in Santa Cruz, California, offered to financially assist any employee with the purchase of a bicycle, he was swamped with requests. Seventy-five of his employees asked for bikes, and the wives of twenty-five more got into the act.

"The parking lot," Lezin found, had taken on "the look of a deserted battlefield." Fewer cars resulted, along with less pollution, reduced auto expenses, and a healthier way to get to work for many of his employees—though the experienced

Lezin did insist that the bikes be ten-speed models because of the hills of Santa Cruz.

The picture is the same across the United States. Major bicycle companies are selling seven million bicycles every year and plan to continue for at least the next few years. According to Schwinn, Huffman, and the other major manufacturers, it will be years before an adult can go into a bicycle shop and buy, on the spot, a new ten-speed model. We must go on a waiting list, because nobody really expected the great fad to turn into a great boom.

Foreign manufacturers can't meet the demand for two-wheelers either. England's Raleigh, France's Peugeot, and Japan's diplomatically named American Eagle make about one third of the bikes sold in the United States, and they expect to remain behind in orders for years to come. Smaller factories in Switzerland and Germany, where many of the hand brakes and gearshift parts are produced, were not expecting the demand, and so huge American companies wait and turn away orders while smaller European factories, unaccustomed to overtime and double shifts, struggle along.

The shortages result from the biggest wave of popularity in the 180-year history of the bicycle. A child's toy? Nearly one half of all production, of all companies, is geared to adult models.

De Sivrac's original *célérifère* was improved with a wooden steering bar and became quite popular in the early 1800s as a "Walkalong." In 1816 Baron von Drais appeared on the streets of Karlsruhe, Germany, with a sleek new "Hobbyhorse," perhaps the first real ancestor of the modern bike. The baron had developed a steerable front wheel. Of course you still just straddled the clumsy machine and pushed it along with leg power, coasting between shoves.

Dennis Johnson took Von Drais's Hobbyhorse and added an adjustable saddle, a cushioned set of armrests, and an improved handlebar, and the popularity of this new "Dandyhorse" zoomed.

A Scotsman who, for his trouble, was ordered from the

streets by police for creating a public disturbance, invented the first pedals. Kirkpatrick MacMillan came up with this ultra-modern idea and the "Wooden horse" was born.

Still the early-day bicycle was a novelty. It was Ernest Michaux, in 1860, who attached the pedals to the front wheel (MacMillan's worked by shafts to the rear wheel) and created the "Bone-shaker," an unsprung monster with huge wheels that clattered and wobbled and banged over the cobblestones of Paris. Pierre Lallement, an employee of Michaux, further improved the Bone-shaker and, after leaving Michaux, was granted the very first United States patent for a bicycle, in the year 1866. The machine that one hundred years or so later was to capture the fancy of the world was officially born.

On September 5, 1971, at the famous Ontario Motor Speedway, a race was flagged off. Every racing fan knows that. But before "the" race, there was another race. The first one was a part of the day's pageantry, a race between teams of "ordinary" riders. This ungainly high-wheeler, invented in 1871 and introduced at the Centennial Exposition, in Philadelphia, in 1876, is still popular among bike-club riders today. A tremendous front wheel, sometimes taller than the man who rides it, has a tiny rear-wheel companion for balance, and stubby pedals at the axle. The rider sits so high that if he should fall, serious injury could result.

Near the turn of the century the wheels on a bicycle became the same size, a chain drive was added, and the "safety" model became the rage. Air-filled rubber tires, ball bearings, coaster brakes, cushion saddles, and adjustable handlebars were introduced, and the "golden age" of bicycles arrived. By 1896, about four million people regularly rode bicycles in the United States, and in the year 1899 there were 312 factories in the United States producing bicycles and bicycle parts.

Some zany models appeared during this first bicycle boom, and a few of them are still in museums. There's the 1896 Columbia bicycle, a ladies' model, with gold-plated metal mounts, ivory handlebar grips, and with the forgotten owner's initials set with diamonds and emeralds. And the Greene and Dyer monocycle, with hand cranks and treadles but no brakes. Another is the sociable tricycle, ridden by two people sitting side by side, not unlike certain modern models. There is the famous dispatch rider's bike, which even bicycle experts have yet to figure out how to ride.

By the 1900s, bicycles looked pretty much as they do today, though gearshifts and other sophisticated inventions hadn't yet appeared. There was a decline in the popularity of bicycles in the early 1900s even though famous names ring out in the sport during this period.

"Mile-A-Minute" Murphy (Charles M. Murphy) stayed with a speeding train, behind a special windbreaking shield, going sixty miles per hour. Murphy accomplished his high-speed ride on June 30, 1899, just before the dawn of the new century. Ralph DePalma, the famous automobile racing driver, got his start racing cycles and worked his way up to more power and speed. He eventually won the famous Indianapolis Speedway race in 1915 (after becoming the sport's most famous loser when, in 1912, he *pushed* his losing car over the finish line in a desperate effort to finish). Wilbur and Orville Wright ran a bicycle repair shop in Dayton, Ohio, and used certain bicycle and chain-drive principles in their airplane. Another aircraft pioneer, Glenn Curtiss, was a bicycle enthusiast early in his life. Henry Ford, R. E. Olds, and George N. Pierce were automotive pioneers addicted to the bicycle first.

Not that record breaking and famous names are a thing of the ancient past in bicycling. On May 17, 1941, for example, Alfred Letourner, a prominent six-day bicycle-racing star, shattered all bicycle speed records when he pedaled a Schwinn Paramount Racer one mile in 33.05 seconds. That's *108.92 miles per hour.*

This speed trial was held on a lonely highway near Bakersfield, California, and participating was famed racing-car driver Ronney Householder.

Famous automobile racing driver Ralph DePalma was first a bicycle racer, as shown here on a Pierce in 1902. (United Savings Helms Athletic Foundation)

Letourner rode behind a shield attached to the rear of Householder's racing car.

The bicycle was equipped with the highest gear ever fitted to a two-wheeler. The front sprocket had fifty-seven teeth, and the rear sprocket had but six, giving the bike a "gear" of 257. The average gear on a bicycle with different speeds today will run from about forty to maybe eighty or ninety.

BALANCE

Have you ever wondered what makes a two-wheeled bicycle, without helper wheels, balance?

A rider balances his bicycle by turning the handlebar, which turns the front wheel from side to side. If the bicycle begins to fall to the right, the rider turns the wheel to the right, in the direction of the fall. The movement is very slight. If the bicycle begins to fall to the left, the same slight movement of the front wheel to the left corrects the balance. When the bicycle reaches a moderate speed, it can be balanced by merely leaning slightly rather than turning the wheel.

TEACHING BALANCE

The best way to teach balance to a newcomer to bicycles is *not* to grasp the seat or back fender and assist as the novice wobbles forward.

First adjust the seat height so that the novice rider's feet barely touch the ground. Then allow him to push forward just as though he were walking one of the early-day Hobbyhorses. When he feels confident, he can lift his feet for a second or so, catching himself instantly if he should begin to fall. In short order he will be coasting farther and farther, and he will have the problem (which is a matter of developing instinct rather than conscious thought) solved.

MODERN BICYCLES

Imports of bikes reached a peak during the 1950s, when the only lightweights available were from overseas, especially from England (accounting for the fact that even now lightweight bicycles are sometimes called "English" models). During the 1960s, though, American manufacturers began to turn out fine, lightweight, geared models, and soon they recaptured the major part of the market. For the first time since 1920, bicycles are once again seriously considered as a means of getting from one place to another.

How fast can they make bikes? One plant, a Schwinn factory in Chicago, is typical. Working on two shifts, they build 5,500 bikes every day, mostly adult ten-speed units. Even at that rate, they do not expect to catch up with the demand for years.

2

Bike Body Construction

How do you plan to use your bike? Decide before you buy, for the modern bicycle has become a specialty item for specific purposes.

If you plan to ride over soft fields or at the beach, or if your bike will be for short rides to school and back or to the store for shopping, get yourself a solid coaster-brake model with fat balloon tires. For these purposes this 45–50-pound model will be efficient and inexpensive, falling in the $25–75 range.

For longer touring or commuting on easy terrain, with no difficult hills, for weekend excursions up to a few miles, for sport or exercise-type riding around the neighborhood every evening, get a three-speed model. This will probably come equipped with hand brakes, though there is a three-speed with coaster-brake hub. Plan to spend from fifty to one hundred dollars at your local bike shop for this 35–40-pound model.

If you plan extended, serious riding over a variety of terrain with steep hills and you don't mind accommodating yourself to a different riding style, buy one of the lightweight five- to fifteen-speed models; ten-speed is the most popular. This is a more high-strung bicycle, which, if you will meet it halfway, will give you a vast improvement in cycling speed and responsiveness. It will weigh as little as fifteen pounds for racing models and cost from one hundred dollars to over four hundred dollars.

Using the ten-speed as a model, let's break down the basic parts of a bike and examine them.

THE FRAME

You could probably use solid-steel dowels for the frame of a bicycle, since this is certainly the heart of the machine and must be strong. The trouble is, solid steel would be heavy and unwieldy and not satisfactory for this use. You could use pipes better suited for plumbing (and a few manufacturers come close), but this is also not satisfactory. It would be too heavy, it would not hold its shape, and the joints would be weak.

The frame of the bike consists of the horizontal *top tube,* a *head tube* at the front, a *seat tube* or *seat mast* parallel to the head tube under the seat, a diagonal *down tube* from the head tube to the *bottom bracket, chain stays* from the bottom bracket to the rear *drop outs,* and *seat stays* from the rear drop outs up to the seat tube, under the seat.

The frame is the single most determining factor in the quality, and thus the cost, of a bike. No matter what else is present, a poor frame means a bike is of questionable quality, but a fine frame will satisfactorily carry along other mistakes in manufacturing judgment. Better yet, a fine frame ordinarily means a fine bike, for no manufacturer likes to spend a lot on one good part and then drape it with inferior parts.

So look at the frame first—especially on the more expensive, lightweight models, where the frame should have just the right blend of stiffness and "give" for perfect response. With a really good frame, the bike will feel almost like an extension of your own body.

SELECTING THE CORRECT FRAME SIZE

Frames are measured from the top of the seat mast to the center of the bottom bracket, and will be from nineteen to twenty-six inches in size. To determine your correct size, straddle the bicycle with your stockinged feet flat on the floor. If you clear the top tube (not the top of the seat tube) by a couple of inches, the size is OK. Too big a frame makes mounting and dismounting difficult, and too small a frame hurts riding efficiency.

FRAME CONSTRUCTION

Olympic teams often use frame material of a special steel alloy called Reynolds 531, made only in England and used on many, many top-quality bikes. Columbus tubing, another steel alloy, comparable to Reynolds 531, is favored by Italian experts.

Frames can be made of straight-gauge, which is good if the material is seamless steel-molybdenum tubing, or double-butted, which is the best.

You won't be able to see it from outside, but frames made of double-butted tubing have walls that are thicker at the ends for strength at the high-stress points and thinner in the middle to reduce weight and add flexibility. If your frame is made of double-butted tubing, it will say so on a sticker on the frame or in the specifications. You'll find straight-gauge frames on bikes running upward from around one hundred dollars and double-butted frames from perhaps one hundred fifty dollars on up.

There are, of course, many other reasonably good types of tubing, and then there are bike frames made with pipes that should have been assigned to carry water to the shower room.

FRAME QUALITY

Although, generally speaking, if the bike is from a known, reputable manufacturer such as Schwinn, Huffy, or some of the other better-known names, the price will give you an idea of frame quality, you can sometimes determine the quality of the frame in better ways. Look at the specification sheet. It might tell you, and it won't lie. Lift the bike. If it feels heavy to you, it might be made from thick tubes welded together. Look for little metal sleeve joints at each frame connection (though certain excellent American bikes do not use this "lugged" construction feature). If the bike has them, it is probably of a better quality, but then check the lugs carefully for a perfectly smooth braze joint. Cracks and globs indicate a poor frame craftsman.

Stand to one side of the bike, grasp the handlebar in one hand and the seat in the other, and tilt the bike away from you. Then place your foot on the bottom bracket and lightly push. The frame should flex slightly, then spring back when you remove the pressure.

Try the same test on an everyday street bike with balloon tires and a "sissy bar" and you'll instantly feel the difference in frame responsiveness. One frame feels "alive" while the other might feel only like good, reliable transportation—which it probably is.

One is a high-bred sports car, the other a family station wagon.

Finally, ride the bicycle in question for one of the very best frame tests. Does it feel "right" to you? Does it feel "good"? Is it comfortable?

FRAME REPAIR

Unless you have a diamond-studded job made of the finest double-butted tubing, forget frame repairs. Breaks, cracks, bends, and other loss of alignment are more difficult and costly to repair than to replace in most cases.

THE FORK

Starting at the top, this device, which holds the front wheel, has a long tube, a fork crown, and then two arms that end with drop outs for the front axle. The long tube at the top is what goes into the head tube of the frame.

Forks are made of solid metal and tubular metal, just like the frame. Experts feel that although the former is the stronger, the latter has enough "give" to soak up the bumps this part of the bicycle must take. Also, the tubular ones, which might be damaged quicker in a crash, can certainly be replaced more cheaply than the entire frame . . . which might have been damaged if the front fork had not had some give to it.

Forks come with a variety of crowns and different bends of the arms (called deflection, or "rake"). The more bend the stronger the crown must be, but the more flexible the fork will be. The less bend, the stiffer, but the crown need not be quite so strong. Generally racers prefer the stiff fork while pleasure riders like the springy, shock-absorbing feeling offered by more flexible forks.

Some bikes carry this to an extreme. Take the "chopper"-style bike with the absurdly extended fork, for example: great shock-absorbing qualities with this model, but of questionable value where strength or precise control is the consideration.

THE HEADSET

Holding the fork tube inside the frame head tube, but allowing it to freely rotate, is the headset. This is a series of nuts, washers, bearings, and races. If the fork seems loose in relation to the frame of the bike, a common symptom, the headset is probably loose. Not many headsets remain in perfect adjustment for the life of the bike, so prepare to keep yours tightened.

HEADSET TIGHTENING

Loosen the lock nut at the very top of the unit, then tighten the threaded top bearing race with your hand if the surface is knurled, or with a large wrench if the surface has flat areas like a nut—not too tight, but just tight enough to stop the looseness in the fork. Retighten the top lock nut.

HEADSET TOO TIGHT

It is a fairly simple matter to loosen the top bearing race by reversing the above process, but chances are, if the headset is too tight the whole unit needs cleaning and lubrication. Bear in mind the order of things, which will probably be, from the top, the lock nut, a washer, the top threaded race, the top bearing, the top set race, then the head tube with the fork tube passing through to the bottom set. The bottom set, going on down, will probably be the bottom set race, the bottom bearing, and the fork crown race. As you can see, everything is snugged down from the top, where it is easy to reach. Other than the fact that you will probably have to tap out the top and bottom set races, which are pressed into the head tube, the whole thing will fall apart when loosened. Have a place other than grass for the bearings to fall, so you won't lose them.

First inspect for any indication of damaged or bent races or worn bearings, which might be causing the binding of the fork in the frame. If everything looks OK, clean in solvent and then lightly grease all the working parts. Be certain, as you reinstall each part, that the set races are even and flush against the edges of the head tube, then tighten the whole thing with the top bearing race and lock it with the top lock nut. Not tight enough to bind the bearings, but hand tighten as snugly as possible without binding.

THE STEM

Between the headset and the handlebar is a small piece called the stem, sometimes also called the gooseneck. At one end of the stem is the clamp that holds the handlebar firmly, and down through the other end is the expander bolt, which is the heart of the stem. This long bolt has a head that protrudes from the top and can be tightened. The tightening action moves a wedge nut at the lower end of the bolt, and clamps the stem to the inside of the fork tube.

You may raise or lower your handlebar by loosening the stem expander bolt (then giving it a light tap with a hammer), then retightening it in the proper position. Always leave a good two and a half inches of the stem inside the fork tube. Most experts agree that the best handlebar height for a lightweight bike with a Maes-type drop bar unit is for the seat to be very slightly higher than the top of the stem.

HANDLEBAR

Generally made of steel or aluminum alloys, handlebars come in a wide variety of sizes and shapes. You can even have them bent to fit you. The handlebar is held to the stem by a fixed bolt and nut, which can be loosened for adjustment or tightened if the handlebar becomes loose in the stem.

Particularly with the Maes-type dropped or "underslung" handlebar, you might wish to install tape for a better and more comfortable grip. Using either a cloth tape or a rubber tape (the type that is thicker in the middle than at the edges), begin about three inches out from the stem. If the tape is the non-sticky type, you can fasten the end with a bit of Scotch tape, then take a couple of turns around the end. Keep the tape snug as you wrap it on, overlapping at least one third. At the bends in the handlebar, overlap more on the inside than on the outside. Go around any hand levers on the handlebar, and at the outside end leave about three inches of tape. Stuff this tape up inside the end of the handlebar, then plug the opening with a cork or a standard handlebar plug.

HANDLEBAR POSITION

The top of the handlebar should be set no higher than the top of the seat. Depending on your own body measurements, the handlebar extension stem may have to be replaced to allow a natural arm position when the back is inclined at about 45° forward.

While leaning forward in the touring position may at first

Handlebars come in all shapes and sizes. Two of the most popular are the drop type, which are generally taped (foreground), and the all-rounder (rear).

feel strange, it will soon prove to be quite comfortable. If not, find the reason why not. If you must stretch, or cramp, or place too much weight on the arms, you might have to adjust the saddle angle, the handlebar angle or height or reach, or even the stem extension.

SEAT (SADDLE)

The saddle of the bicycle is attached by a heavy wire frame and a bracket to the seat post, which is held by a bolt inside the seat tube of the frame. Seats come in an even wider variety than handlebars, from the zany "banana" types

Saddles are shaped for the job as well. In the foreground is the cutaway, racing-type saddle, and to the rear is the mattress-type, softer and not quite so "professional."

made of bright colors and metal-flaked, to the thin, hard, cutaway, springless racing saddles used by the professionals. Where these latter ones do not look very comfortable, the rider is not sitting on his pedaling muscles as he does on some of the broader ones, and so less work is needed and chafing is reduced to a minimum. You'll have to settle on the type you like best by trial and error, since that part of our anatomy differs with each one of us. You might start, however, with the modern mattress type, which combines a bit of the cutaway with a good deal more padding.

If the seat rocks back and forth, fit a box wrench on the

tightening nut and snug it up. Most people like their bike seat to be about level, but you might experiment by tilting it slightly back and then slightly forward to find the most comfortable riding position.

If the seat swivels from side to side or slides down into the seat tube of the frame, place it at the proper level and tighten the bolt on the seat tube. What is the proper level? See "Saddle Position," below.

If you are having trouble getting the seat post to remain firm in the seat tube, you could have a post that's too small. They come in different sizes. In this case, either get a shim to firm up the fit, or get a new seat post.

SADDLE POSITION

Set the nose of the saddle about two inches behind an imaginary line drawn vertically through the center of the bottom bracket. Then, with the pedal in the lowest position, raise the saddle until the heel (in stockinged feet) just rests on the pedal, with the leg straight, when seated in a natural position on the saddle. When the ball of the foot is placed on the pedal in proper riding position, the leg will have a very slight bend.

3

Chains, Sprockets, and Pedals

Your bicycle will operate with many ills, but if the ill is with the chain the operating days are numbered, for if the chain fails operation stops. This is the connection between the power of your muscles and the turning rear wheel. No matter what type of bike, or what gear selection, the chain is the key to power transmission.

The chain is the most hard-working and the dirtiest part of the bicycle. Preventative maintenance of this part is a necessity, for if the chain becomes caked with dirt or rust or if it is operated without lubrication, it will fail. If it stretches, and it eventually will, even with the best of care, it will not operate as efficiently.

Generally children's bikes and adult bikes up to the three-speed models have a chain with a master connecting link. The oversized chain plate of this link can be popped off and snapped back on so that the chain can be removed for maintenance or repair. Ten-speed-model chains do not have this link, and so work on this chain will require a simple chain tool for punching out and replacing rivets on whatever link you select.

THROWN CHAIN

If your bike is a single-speed or a three-speed model, refer to the section in this chapter on loose chains. If your bike is a ten-speed model, refer to the chapter on Gears, the section on chain throwing from either high or low gear.

NOISY OR DIRTY CHAIN

You might try cleaning the chain by soaking a rag in solvent, then holding the rag around the chain as you turn the pedals (in reverse on all but the coaster-brake models, with the rear wheel raised and the chain moving forward on the latter). If the chain is *really* dirty, remove it and soak it in a solvent bath until it is clean. Swish it around and flex it while in the bath so that the solvent can get in between the chain plates and rollers.

OILING THE CHAIN

The idea is to get a thin coat of oil between the plates and the rollers, with as little oil as possible elsewhere, since oil attracts dirt and grit like a magnet, and dirt and grit are chain killers. The way to do it is to drip oil, drop by drop only, onto the chain plates while the chain is moving. Do this at the front of the front chain sprocket while the chain is moving (in reverse if possible, forward on coaster-brake models). *Gentle* with the oil. Finally move the chain through a clean rag to spread the oil and to soak up the excess.

LOOSE CHAIN

On the single-speed and three-speed models, a loose chain can be tightened by merely loosening the rear wheel nuts and moving the wheel back slightly in the rear drop outs. Then tighten the nuts in the new position. The chain should have about one half inch of flex at the correct tension. Be sure to tighten the right wheel nut first, then align the wheel so that

A typical chain tool in operation, punching out the rivet that holds the *dérailleur* chain together at each link. This screw-type tool can be used either on the bicycle or in a vise. (Schwinn Bicycle Company)

the rim is evenly between the chain stays before final tightening of both nuts. You will probably have to loosen the coaster-brake bracket before moving the rear wheel on single-speed bikes.

On ten-speed models, the tension of the chain is regulated by the *dérailleur,* and so if the chain is loose with all adjustments made (see chapter on Gears), a link must be removed. This is a fairly simple matter of driving out rivets, removing a link, and refastening the chain, but a small chain tool is a

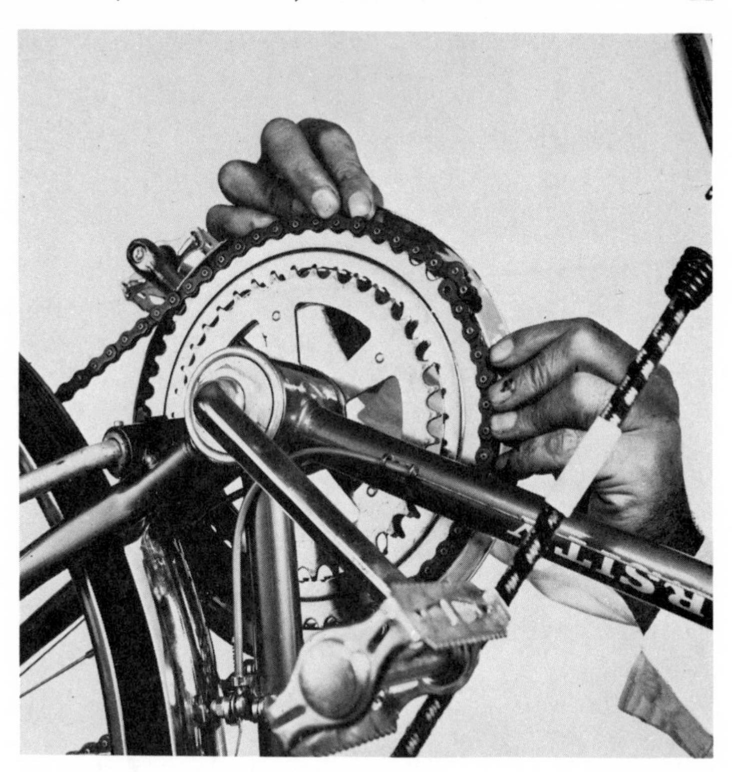

To determine the proper length of chain on a dérailleur-model bicycle, fit the chain onto the large front and rear sprockets and through the roller cage. Draw the chain tight around the front sprocket, where the roller cage pivots to its maximum. Allow one-half to a full link of extra chain for fitting the chain together. (Schwinn Bicycle Company)

necessity. Get the tool at your local bike shop for a couple of bucks before you try any "home mechanic" methods.

WARPED OR STICKING LINK

If your chain seems to "thump" or "click" at one spot as it passes over a sprocket or through a dérailleur, or if it kinks

When removing dérailleur chain, place link and rivet on chain-tool guide. Turn tool handle enough to partially push out rivet. Then remove chain from tool and slightly bend chain to unhook link from rivet. (Schwinn Bicycle Company)

and won't straighten, you probably have a jamming link. Perhaps some dirt has worked into the link, or perhaps it is dry. First of all, put a drop of oil on the offending link. That could fix things.

Try loosening the link very slightly with a chain tool, or even with the blade of a small screwdriver, and then add a bit more oil. If the link is warped or bent, replace it.

To install a chain link, partially press out a rivet, hook in end link, then press in rivet with chain tool. Bend chain from side to side at these points to free any tight links. (Schwinn Bicycle Company)

WORN CHAIN

After a few years the chain of your bike, one part that works under the worst conditions, is going to simply wear out. When it reaches the point where it flexes from side to side, where it has just too much play, where each link seems loose and sloppy, when the chain "clicks and groans," it is time to install a new one. On a single-speed or a three-speed, flip off the

To check for too short a chain, shift chain onto large front sprocket, then try to shift chain to large *rear* sprocket. If chain tends to strain and bend rear dérailleur as shown here, lengthen chain accordingly. (Schwinn Bicycle Company)

master link and drop the old chain, guide on the new one, and snap the new master link in place. Then adjust the rear wheel. On a ten-speed, get a new length of chain slightly longer than you think you need, thread it through, and then, when you are certain the chain is installed correctly, rivet the connecting link with your chain tool.

Then, in both cases, properly oil the chain.

A freewheel sprocket cluster on the bike and ready to go.

And speaking of chains, touring cyclists always include a master link or an extra few links, with a chain tool, in their toolbox. This equipment is light in weight and easily carried and can save you a long walk to the nearest service facility.

SPROCKETS

The sprockets on a bicycle are the wheels with teeth that fit into the links of the chain. On a single-speed or a three-speed model, there is a sprocket in front with pedals attached, and one at the rear wheel. On multi-speed models with dérailleurs, there can be one, two, or even three sprockets in front, and up to five different-sized ones in a freewheel cluster at the

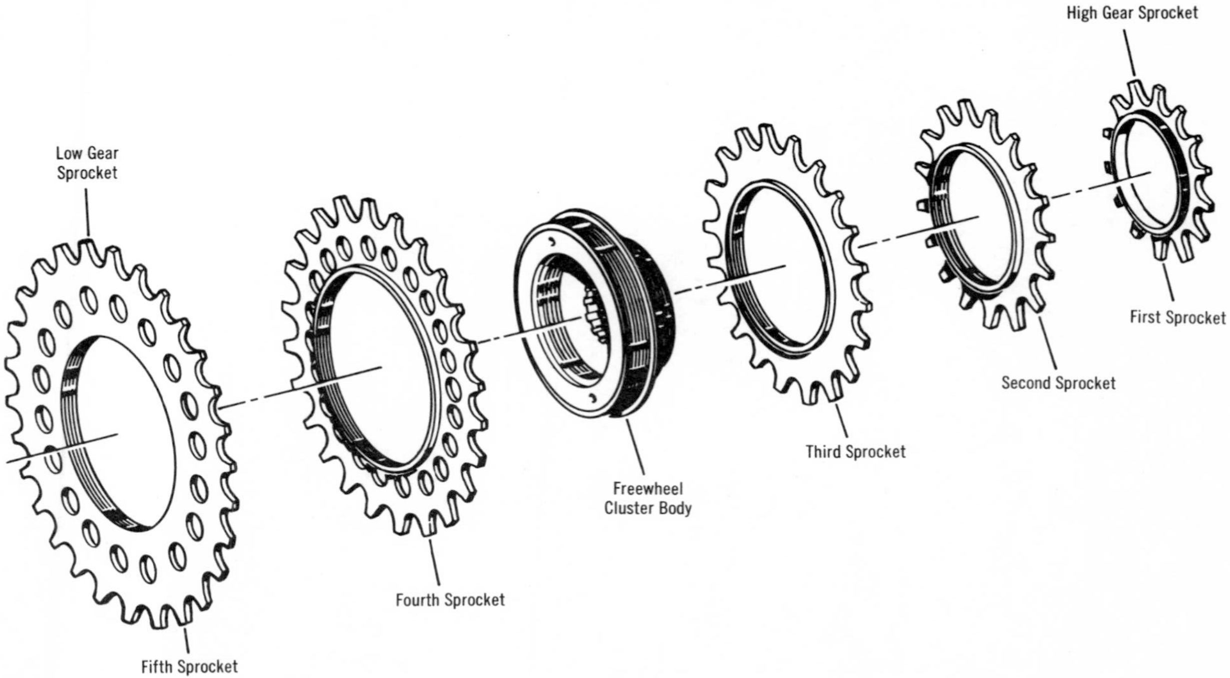

Low Gear
Sprocket
Fifth Sprocket
Fourth Sprocket
Freewheel
Cluster Body
Third Sprocket
Second Sprocket
High Gear Sprocket
First Sprocket

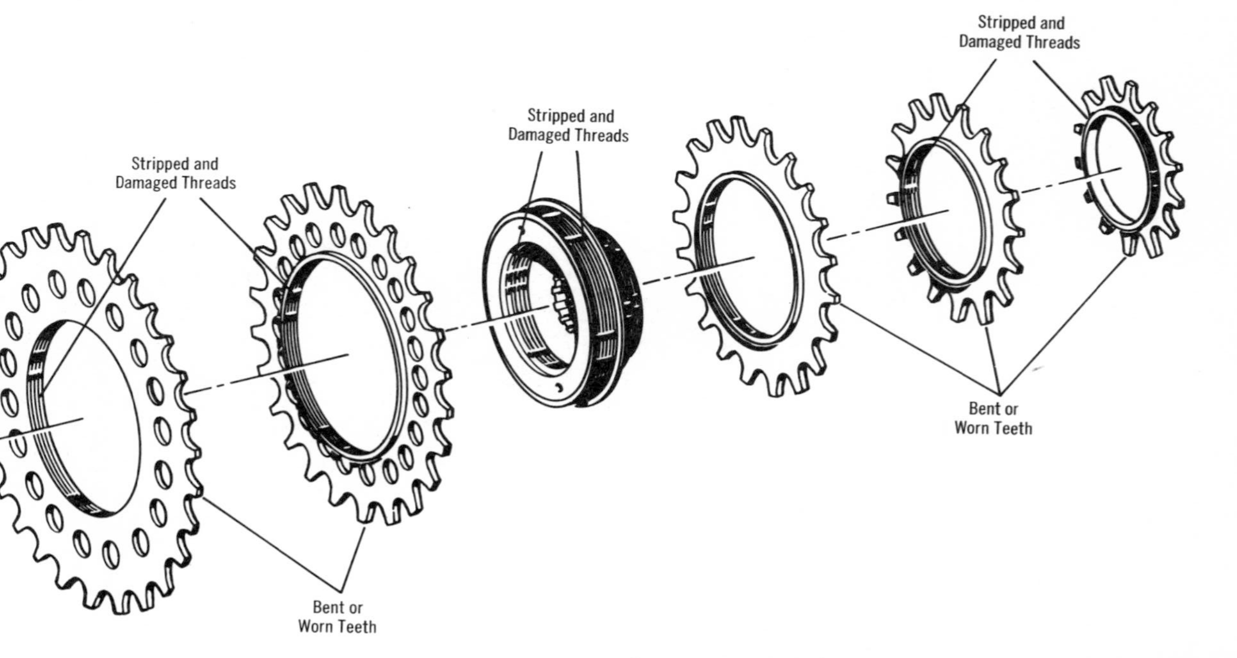

Drawing shows an exploded view of a freewheel cluster. (Schwinn Bicycle Company)

rear wheel. A combination of one in front and one at the rear gives one speed, where two in the front and five at the rear offers ten speeds, and three in front and five at the rear gives fifteen speeds. The chain is guided by dérailleurs from one sprocket to another, front and rear, until the gear ratio desired is reached.

On one- and three-speed models the sprockets will probably operate forever, and on a ten-speed model your chances are almost as good. Generally the problems in this area will be with the dérailleurs or the chain. Still, it is possible that a bad chain will have worn the teeth on the freewheel or the front sprocket.

Obviously, if a tooth is broken off or if the teeth are badly worn (or if you merely want a different combination of gears), the sprocket must be replaced. But always examine other possible causes before going to the sprockets if trouble develops.

In one sense, however, a bike is like a television set. Replace one tube, and this changes the "balance" which the working team of tubes has achieved, and so other tubes may soon need replacing. On your bike, a change of a chain can upset the fine balance among chain, sprockets, and dérailleurs, so examine everything closely. And *plan* on adding a new chain if for some reason you have changed your freewheel or front sprocket, for an older chain is almost certain to act up on a new sprocket.

PEDALS AND CRANKS

Pedals are the metal-and-rubber platforms (or all-metal in the "rattrap" racing models with toe clips for better "around" pedaling) attached to the crank. The crank is attached to and turns the front sprocket when you push with the balls of your feet. So what else is new? Well, the *way* you push these pedals, for one thing.

You will go much farther, with much less fatigue, if you learn to pedal properly. The idea is not to push the pedals *down,* but to push them *around.* Think "around" as you

The large, flat-sided link in the center is the "master" link, for removing the chain.

pedal. This is also called "ankling." Help the thrust of your left leg with a little final push of the right foot. It is amazing how this proper pedaling will increase efficiency—and decrease fatigue.

The type of pedals and cranks has probably been determined for you, since they were one of the parts already installed on the bike when you bought it, and you probably gave little thought to these items. No problem. The bike maker has installed the best pedal and crank for the model, though these parts do vary. On the most expensive bicycles they are made up of several parts with, for example, a separate axle through the bottom hanger. On some bikes the crank is one piece, turned at the center into an axle, then pedals are attached at each end after the crank has been put through the bottom bracket.

Pedals are more complicated than they look, but they will

probably work on forever, or until the rubber parts are worn and drop off (at which point, replace the whole pedal). Inside a pedal is an axle with some bearings at each end, so grease these parts from time to time, especially if they make a noise or begin to act sticky. Replacement pedals, if you want the finest, can cost up to twenty-five dollars a pair. Three- or four-dollar ones will probably do just as well, unless you are planning to enter the Tour de France.

4

Brakes

A bicycle is driven forward by the action of your legs moving pedals, which move cranks, which turn a front sprocket, which pulls a chain, which turns a rear sprocket, which is attached to the rear wheel. And so the wheel turns and the bike moves.

But what makes it stop?

COASTER BRAKE

On one-, three-, and certain five-speed models is a foot-operated coaster brake, which shifts the drive to the wheel when the pedals are moving forward, shifts to freewheeling when the pedals are stopped, and applies a rear-wheel brake in the hub when the pedals are pushed backward. It is an efficient, long-lasting piece of equipment that, if properly lubricated, may *never* need attention.

There are three reasons why every single bicycle doesn't use a coaster brake: it offers a much smaller gear selection or none at all, it is unhandy to repair should the need arise, and modern riders of ten-speed models prefer hand brakes on both wheels to an internal coaster brake on one wheel. Hand brakes are also efficient and much easier to service.

Typical "side-pull" brake mechanism.

There is a very important oil nipple on the rear hub, which admits lubrication to the inner mechanisms of both coaster brake and three-speed gears. Use this oil nipple, once a month or more often—two or three drops. If problems develop with the coaster brake (and if they do it is an indication that replacement parts will be needed rather than simple adjustments), take the wheel off and to a bike repair shop. You can't ignore brake problems, but the coaster brake is a difficult thing to get involved with. The most efficient way, and probably cheaper in the long run, is to let somebody who really understands do it for you.

HAND BRAKES, CENTER, SIDE-PULL, AND EXPANDER

Much like a disc brake on an automobile, the hand, or "caliper," brake on a bicycle, when applied, squeezes brake pads onto the wheel rim and the friction stops the wheel.

Typical "center-pull" brake mechanism.

Hand brakes come in two main types: center-pull and side-pull. Both work the same way. You squeeze a lever on the handlebar and this pulls on a cable, which in turn pulls on the brake mechanism on the wheel. Rubber brake shoes close and the wheel stops turning. On one, an activating cable pulls from the *center* of the brake mechanism, and on the other, a lever on one *side* is pulled by the main cable.

Aluminum-alloy brake mechanisms mean higher quality and less weight.

On both types, spring-loaded arms return the shoes to a position away from the wheel rims when you relax pressure on the hand lever.

Or should.

BRAKE-SHOE DRAG, CENTER-PULL

If one brake shoe continues to rub the wheel rim after you have released the hand lever, it is likely that the whole brake

Brake lever on the handlebar. This lever has an inward-projecting extension for easy reach when the rider is holding center section of Maes-type bar.

mechanism has shifted on its long holding bolt. Merely loosen the holding nut, and with your hands gently shift the mechanism until both brake shoes clear the rim. Then tighten the holding nut.

If *both* brake shoes are dragging, first check the hand lever to be certain it is in the released position. Then check the cable to be certain it is not sticking in its housing and holding the rubber shoes against the wheel. Oil will probably cure any cable sticking problems or any lever hang-ups.

Then try a little oil on the two pivot bolts holding the brake arms. To work the oil in, move the arms manually. At the same time, examine the arms to be sure they aren't bent and rubbing against each other. They should not touch, so, if they do, you might very gently move them apart with the blade of a small screwdriver. Badly bent arms should, of course, be replaced. During your examination check for a broken return

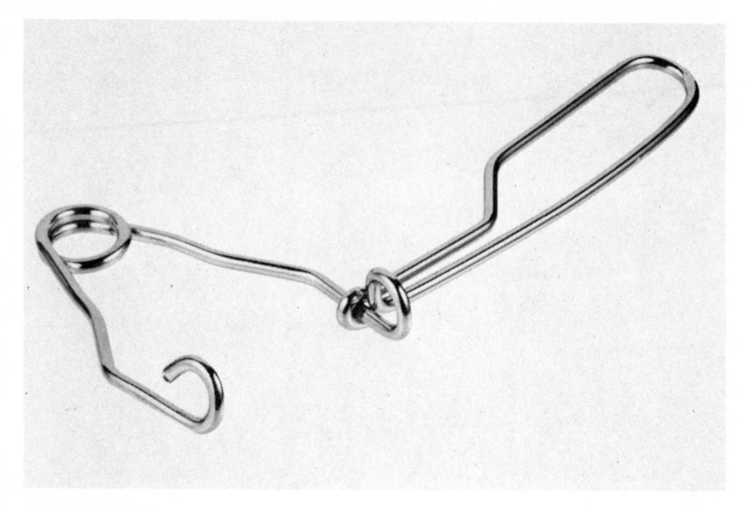

A "third hand" tool, for holding brake shoes firmly against the wheel rim, freeing both hands to adjust cables. (Schwinn Bicycle Company)

spring, or bent pivot bolts, which could also be causing the drag of the brake shoes.

BRAKE-SHOE DRAG, SIDE-PULL

If one brake shoe continues to rub the wheel rim after you have released pressure on the hand lever, it is likely that the whole brake mechanism has shifted on its pivot bolt. Loosen the pivot-bolt nut, and with your hands gently shift the mechanism until both brake shoes clear the rim. Then tighten the pivot-bolt nut.

If the brake shoes keep coming back to the same position

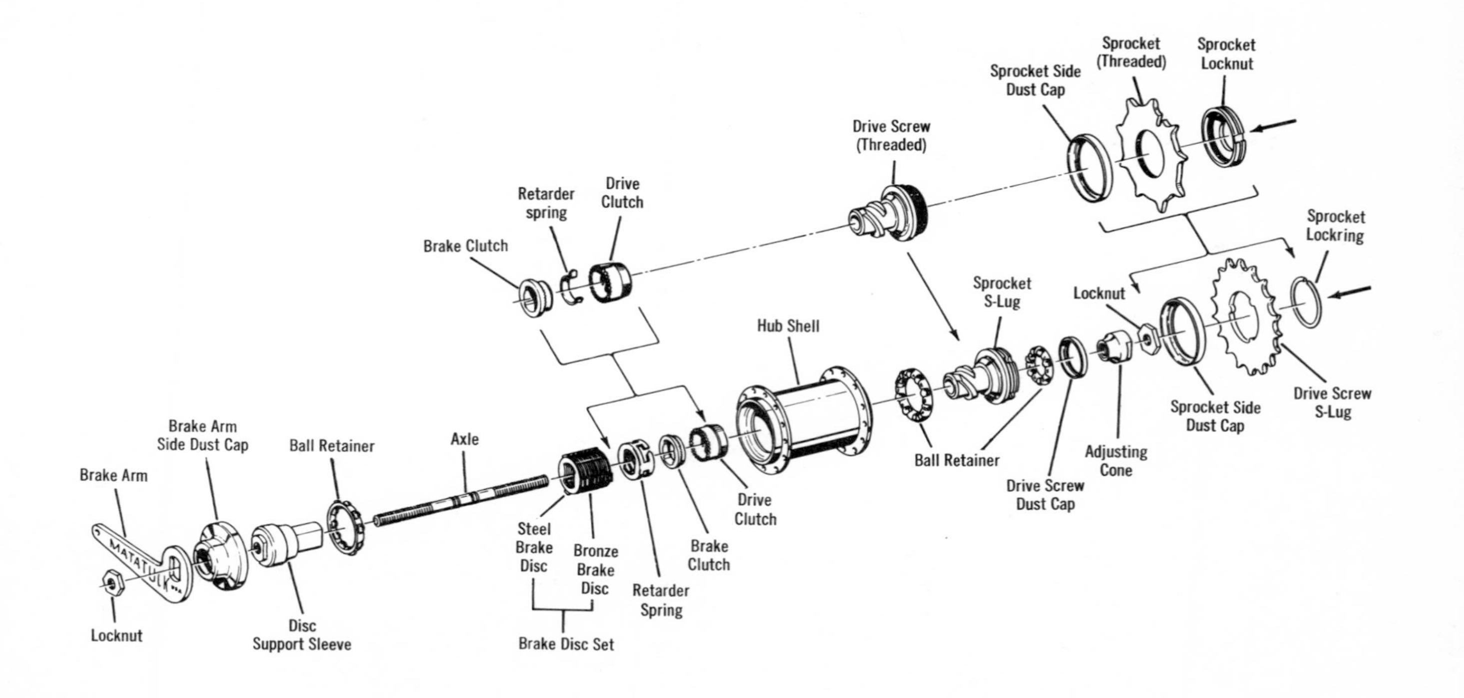
Sprocket Side Dust Cap
Sprocket (Threaded)
Sprocket Locknut
Drive Screw (Threaded)
Retarder spring
Drive Clutch
Brake Clutch
Sprocket Lockring
Sprocket S-Lug
Locknut
Hub Shell
Brake Arm Side Dust Cap
Ball Retainer
Axle
Brake Arm
Drive Screw S-Lug
Sprocket Side Dust Cap
Adjusting Cone
Ball Retainer
Drive Screw Dust Cap
Drive Clutch
Brake Clutch
Steel Brake Disc
Bronze Brake Disc
Retarder Spring
Locknut
Disc Support Sleeve
Brake Disc Set

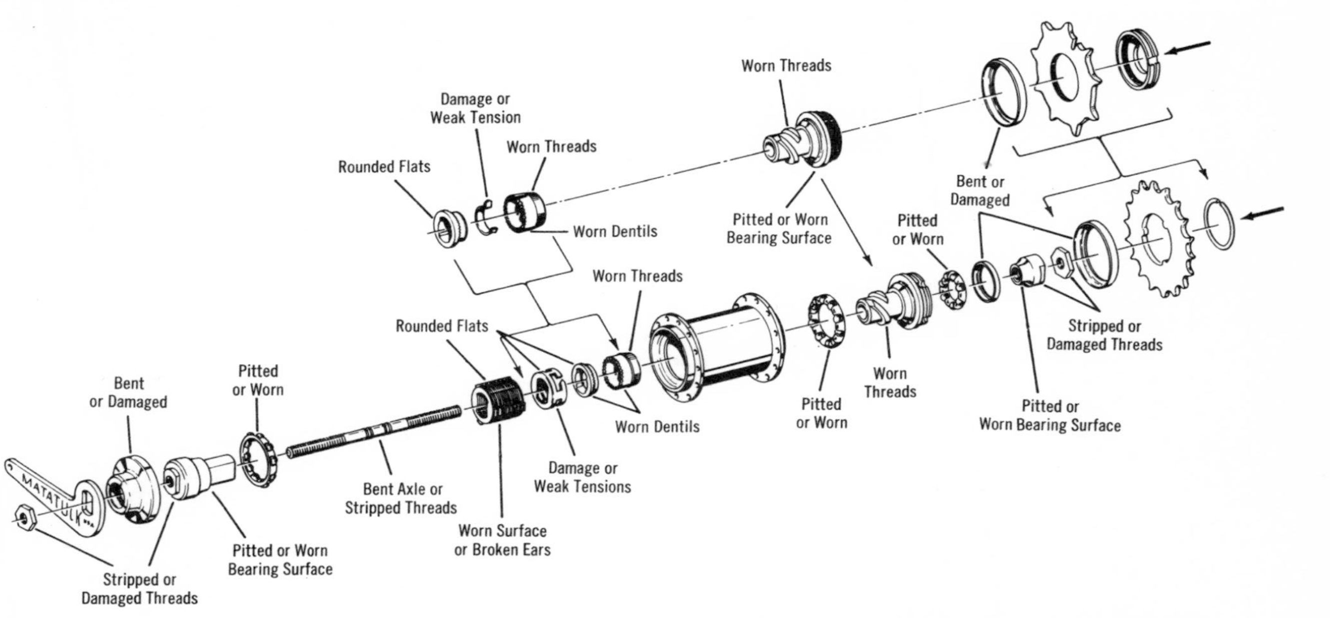

Exploded view, and check list for single-spaced rear hubs with coaster brakes. Mattatuck-Hawthorne-New Departure-Nakai model. (Schwinn Bicycle Company)

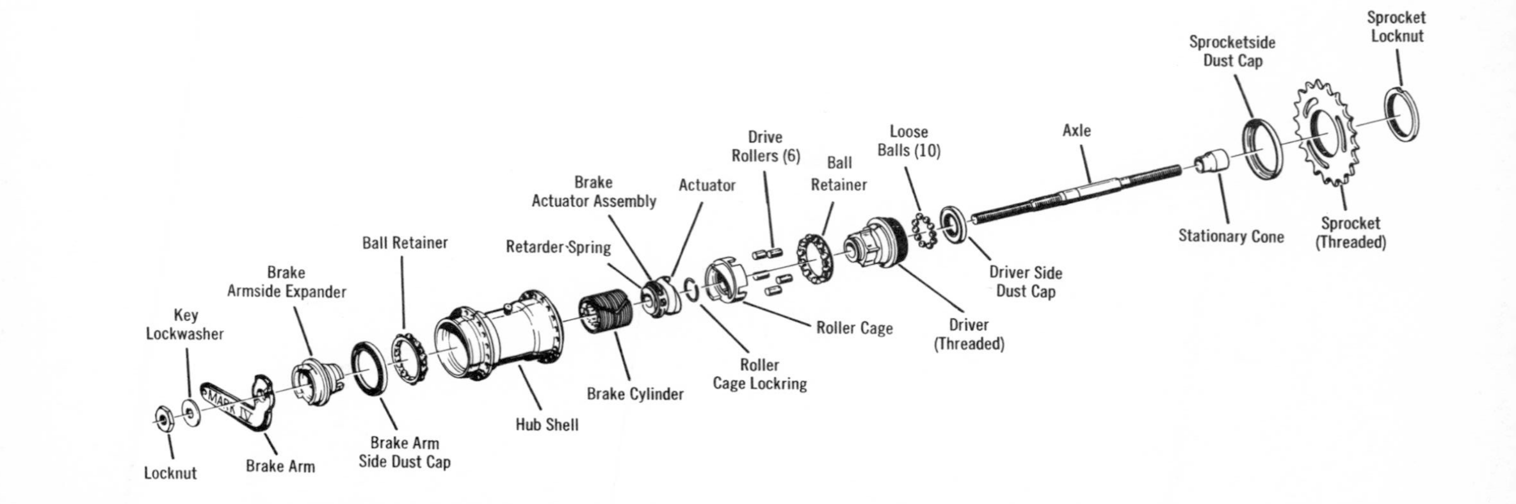
Sprocket Locknut
Sprocketside Dust Cap
Sprocket (Threaded)
Stationary Cone
Axle
Loose Balls (10)
Driver Side Dust Cap
Driver (Threaded)
Drive Rollers (6)
Ball Retainer
Roller Cage
Actuator
Brake Actuator Assembly
Roller Cage Lockring
Retarder-Spring
Brake Cylinder
Hub Shell
Ball Retainer
Brake Arm Side Dust Cap
Brake Armside Expander
Key Lockwasher
Brake Arm
Locknut
MARK IV

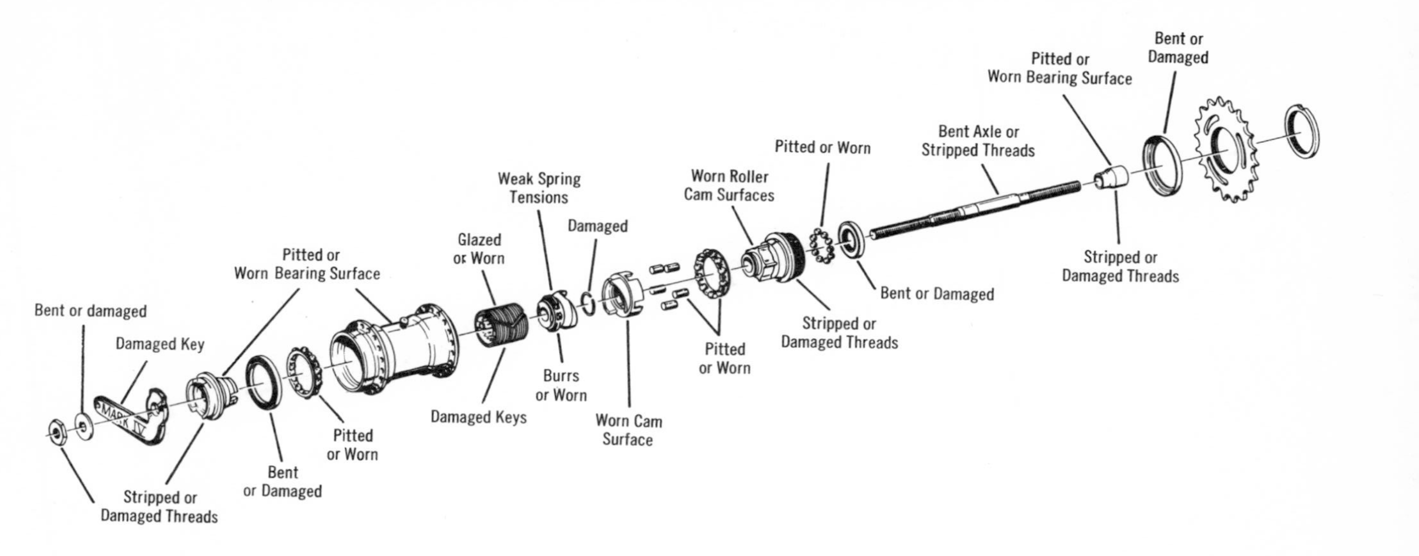

Exploded view and check list for single spaced rear hubs with coaster brakes. Mark IV model. (Schwinn Bicycle Company)

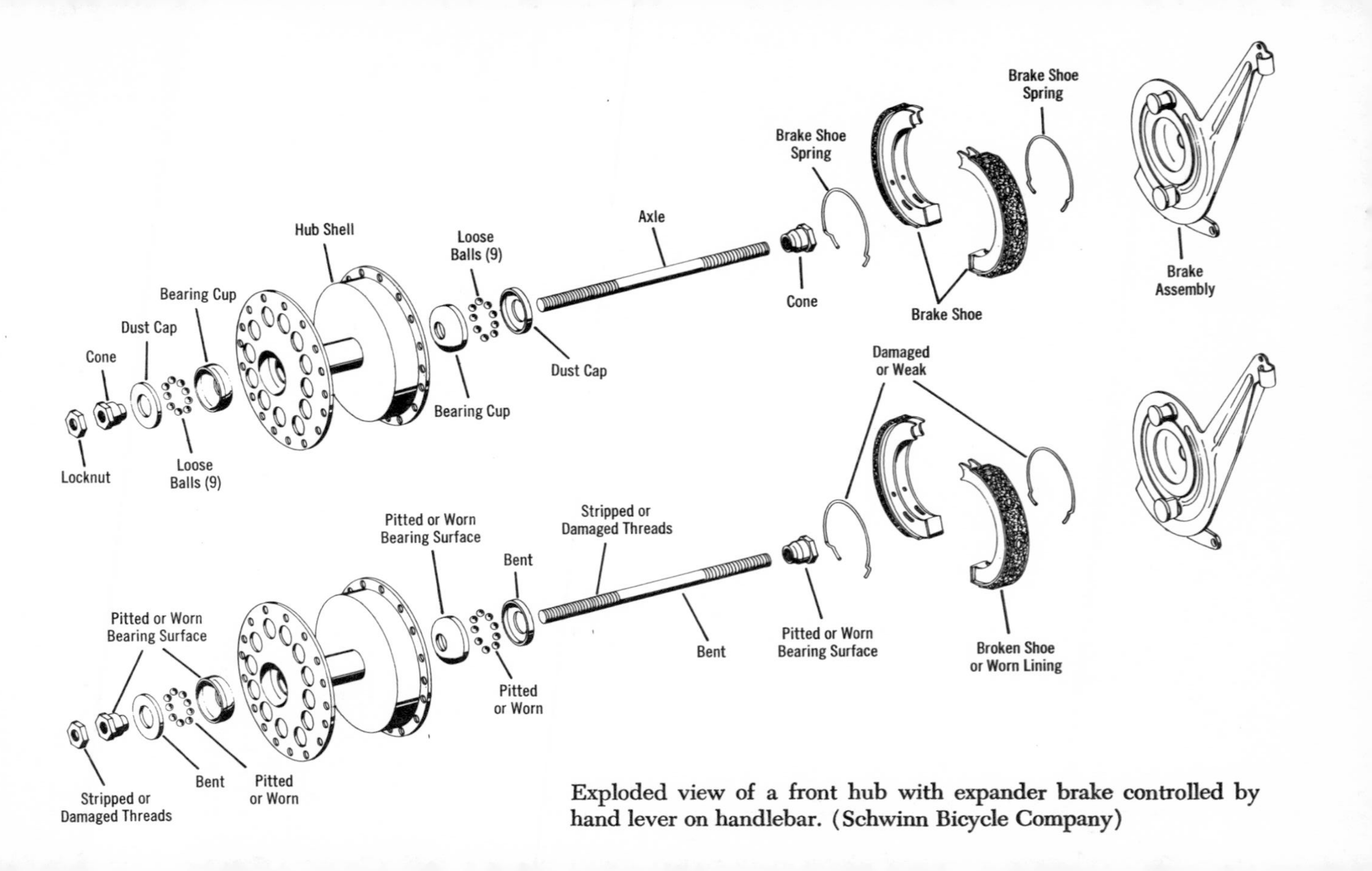

Exploded view of a front hub with expander brake controlled by hand lever on handlebar. (Schwinn Bicycle Company)

no matter how many times you adjust the mechanism, try bending the spring that spreads the inner and outer arms.

If both brake pads are dragging, first check the hand lever to be certain it is in the released position. Then check the cable to be certain it is not sticking in its housing and holding the shoes against the wheel rim. Oil will probably cure either of these problems.

Check the lock nuts on the pivot bolt to be certain they are not squeezing the brake arms together. A drop or two of oil on the pivot bolt followed by hand-working the brake arms might cure the problem. Be certain the brake arms are not rubbing together because of damage to one or the other. If this is the problem, you might cure it by wedging them apart gently with a screwdriver blade, but work slowly and carefully, and if a little force doesn't do it, plan to replace parts instead.

LOOSE BRAKES

Tighten loose brakes, both center-pull and side-pull, by adjusting the cable tension. This is done by loosening the lock ring on the brake cable, tightening the adjusting sleeve, then retightening the lock ring.

BRAKE SHOES

The shoes, which are generally of rubber, are clamped in brake blocks, which, by one of two ways, are attached to the brake arms on the mechanism.

Brake shoes will be the standard type (held onto the *slotted* end of the standard brake arm by a bolt) or the eyebolt type (held to the *tapered* end of the brake arm by a clamp).

The more popular, standard type can be adjusted up and down so that it exactly meets the rim vertically, and forward or backward for a perfect horizontal match.

The eyebolt type of shoe can be adjusted in both these directions, and also can be pivoted to match a more flaring wheel rim squarely (if necessary).

A correctly adjusted brake shoe should hit the rim as squarely as possible. Some riders prefer the front of the shoe to make contact with the rim first, a "toe-in" condition, but never adjust the shoes so that the rear hits first.

BRAKE NOISE

If a coaster brake squeals or screams, head immediately for the bike repair shop, for something is wrong. But if hand brakes squeal, don't panic. Many of them do, and yet the brakes are perfectly OK. If you really can't stand the noise, check the rim of the offending wheel. It could be dirty or dented. Clean it or straighten it. It could be that the rubber of the shoes is worn down to the metal brake blocks, and a metal-to-metal contact is causing the noise. This situation should be remedied immediately with new shoes.

With hand brakes, on a wet day, try to remember to apply them lightly a short distance before you really need them. This wipes off the moisture on the wheel rim so that when you apply them firmly they won't slip.

EXPANDER BRAKES

Even more like standard automobile brakes, except that you apply them by hand rather than foot, is the expander-type bicycle brake. Brake shoes open when a hand lever is squeezed and a brake cable pulled, and rubbing against a brake drum causes the wheel to stop. This type brake is simply adjusted by loosening the lock nut on the cable, turning the adjusting barrel nut to the proper adjustment, then tightening the lock nut.

5

Gears

You can laugh, but it's true. The Walkalong of the 1800s, and the Hobbyhorse, the Dandy-horse, and the Swiftwalker, which followed, had something in common with modern bikes up to recently. That is that they were *pushed* along by leg power, and so are modern single-speed bikes pushed from time to time.

Take a long hill, for example. Perhaps not until the very last minute, until the pains started in the legs, but eventually most of us slowed, wobbled, and finally stepped off. The rest of the way to the top was walking and pushing.

Not any more! In fact, when the three-speed began to replace the single-speed bike, it was like going from a truck to a passenger car, and then along came the lightweight five- and ten- and fifteen-speed models. Suddenly the *three-speed* was the truck.

A hill you could barely climb with a single-speed was much easier with a three-speed, and with a ten-speed the same hill can be made with no strain at all.

A long ride in the country on yesterday's single-speed, a ride that brought you home gasping and promising yourself to look into your own general physical condition, is a breeze on a ten-speed. For the gears on a modern bicycle are not just

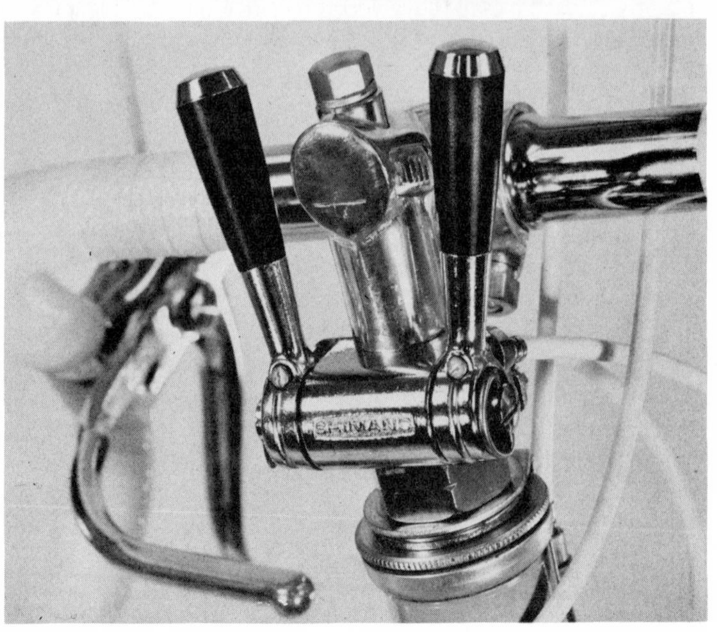
SHIMANO

extra toys to raise the price, or fancy "goodies" to help sell the unit. They are precision-made bicycle transmissions that do just as much for your legs as the automobile transmission does for the engine.

The single-speed has a somewhat larger front sprocket and a somewhat smaller sprocket at the rear hub, and around them passes a chain. If the front sprocket could be replaced with a larger one, or the rear with a smaller one, the result would be a much higher speed, but unfortunately a greater effort of the legs would be required to reach this speed. Enlarging the size of the "driven" gear (the rear sprocket) is like putting a car into "low," great power for hard work such as uphill climbing but lower speeds resulting.

Carrying this thought further, the problems are (1) you cannot simply change the sprockets on a country road and (2) even if you could there are limits. Too large a pedal sprocket and you could not develop the power in your legs to turn it

Three types of lever shifters for moving the chain from sprocket to sprocket. (The Huffman Company)

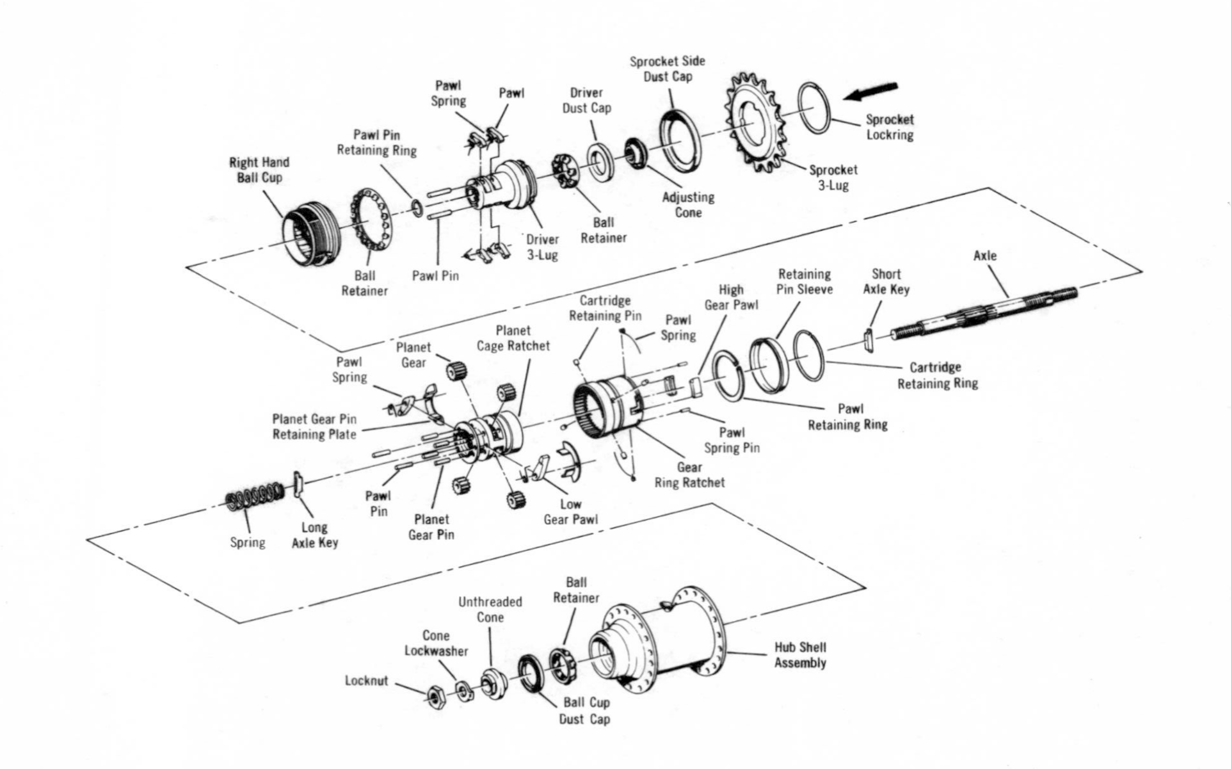
Sprocket Side Dust Cap
Pawl Spring
Pawl
Driver Dust Cap
Sprocket Lockring
Pawl Pin Retaining Ring
Right Hand Ball Cup
Sprocket 3-Lug
Adjusting Cone
Ball Retainer
Driver 3-Lug
Ball Retainer
Pawl Pin
Axle
Retaining Pin Sleeve
Short Axle Key
High Gear Pawl
Cartridge Retaining Pin
Pawl Spring
Planet Cage Ratchet
Planet Gear
Pawl Spring
Cartridge Retaining Ring
Pawl Retaining Ring
Planet Gear Pin Retaining Plate
Pawl Spring Pin
Gear Ring Ratchet
Pawl Pin
Planet Gear Pin
Low Gear Pawl
Spring
Long Axle Key
Ball Retainer
Unthreaded Cone
Cone Lockwasher
Hub Shell Assembly
Locknut
Ball Cup Dust Cap

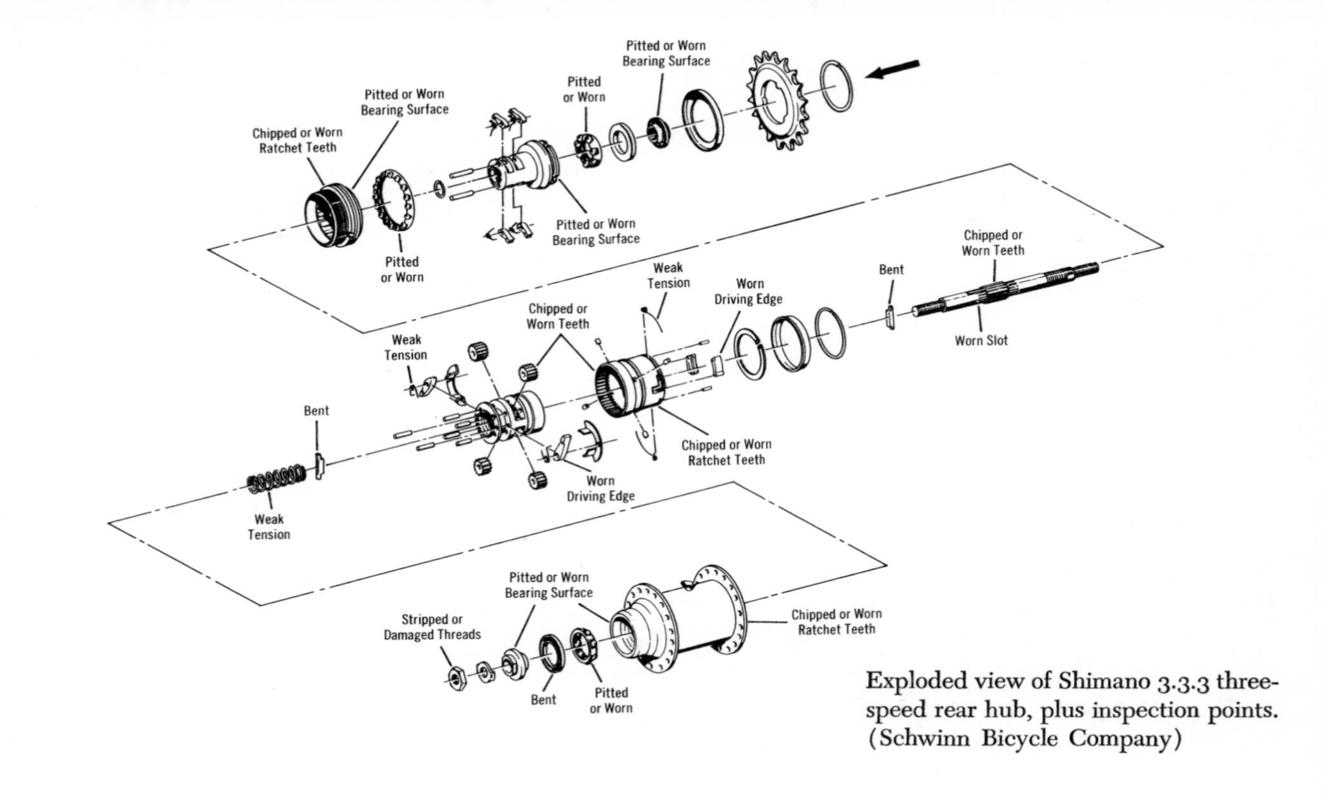

Exploded view of Shimano 3.3.3 three-speed rear hub, plus inspection points. (Schwinn Bicycle Company)

Another view of a three-speed rear hub, on the bicycle. To adjust, set gear selector in center position, then turn adjusting barrel (after loosening lock nut) to align shoulder of indicator spindle with the end of the axle (as seen through "window" in rear-axle-nut extension). (Schwinn Bicycle Company)

(even though a tremendous speed would be the theoretical result). Too small a pedal sprocket and you would have to pedal very fast to move at all (though the developed torque would be great).

But if you *could* change sprockets, either front, rear, or both, and if they *were* of a size to efficiently use pedal power, you would be able to tame the toughest hill by lower gearing, and travel very fast on the level by higher gearing, all with relative ease.

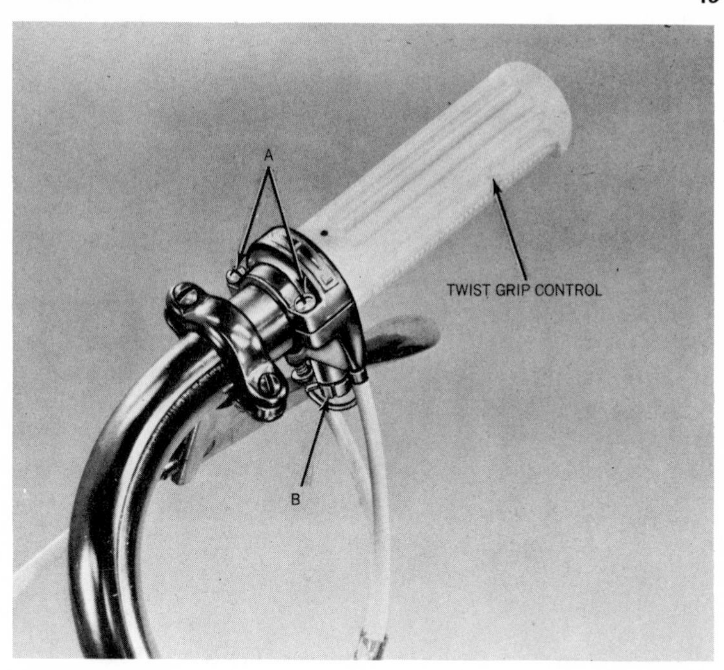

Typical twist grip control for shifting a three-speed hub. Note high, low and marked standard position in center. Screws A are holding screws, while B adjusts the tension of the shifter. It should be loose enough to shift, but firm, with an amount of resistance. (The Huffman Company)

As you have already seen, so you can with the current three-, five-, ten-, and fifteen-speed bicycles.

And where we have been reading good American names like Schwinn and Huffy, exotic names now begin to enter the bicycle picture: Shimano, Huret Allvit, Sturmey-Archer, and Campagnolo are a few. Most of the gearing devices used on American bikes are foreign-made.

Here's what they are, how they work, and what to do if they stop working:

THREE-SPEED MODELS

With either a twist grip to shift gears, or a lever, the gearing on the three- and certain five-speed models is cable-controlled and *within* the rear hub. Where they are relatively trouble-free, they can get out of adjustment due to cable stretch, though once "broken in" this is not much of a problem. And adjustment, when needed, is simple.

Your three-speed bicycle will probably have one of the three-speed hubs that make up a majority of all the three-speed hubs in the world. In no particular order, these are:

1. Sturmey-Archer AW (wide ratio);
2. Sturmey-Archer TCW (combining three-speed mechanism with coaster brake);
3. Shimano 3.3.3.

The three-speed hub provides a low-, a normal-, or intermediate-, and a high-speed combination, as well as freewheeling for coasting. The five-speed adds two more combinations. All the moving parts are inside the rear hub, with the gear selection controlled by a cable connected to the shifter.

A rule: never shift a three-speed while pedaling forward. Shifting of this type of bicycle transmission should be done while the bike is moving but freewheeling.

STURMEY-ARCHER AW AND TCW HUBS

The gears of these models are synchronized at the factory with the shifting lever or twist grip. If the adjustment is no longer correct due to cable stretching or other cause, proceed as follows:

Set the gear-speed indicator on the shifter at N or II or on the mid-range mark, whatever it might be.

Release the lock nut, and screw the cable connector at the rear wheel until the end of the indicator rod is exactly aligned with the extreme end of the axle (as seen through the "window" in the right-hand nut).

Then tighten the lock nut.

Three-speed rear hub on bicycle, ready for action. Note knurled cable connector adjusting device, and lock nut, as well as indicator window (on this model)

This procedure will realign the gearshift lever or twist grip with the position of the gears in the hub.

LOOSE WHEEL

If the rear axle nuts are tight but the wheel is loose ("end play," like a loose wheel bearing), the bearing adjustment should be tightened. To do this, loosen the lock nut on the *left side* of the hub, adjust the left bearing cone suitably, then retighten the lock nut. The right-hand cone is fixed in the Sturmey-Archer models. Do not overtighten the bearing cone. Remember: a properly adjusted wheel bearing will still have a little "play" at the rim.

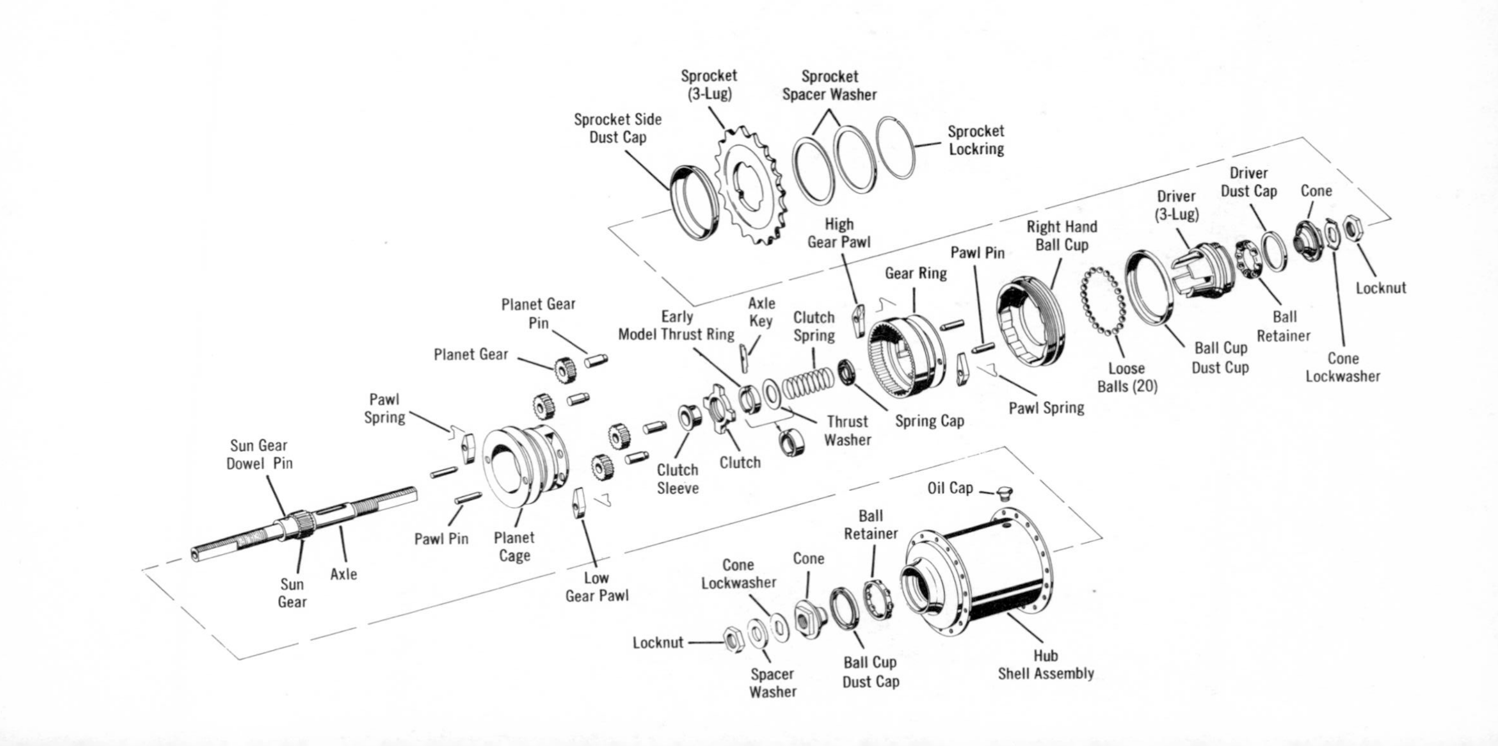
Sprocket Side Dust Cap
Sprocket (3-Lug)
Sprocket Spacer Washer
Sprocket Lockring
High Gear Pawl
Gear Ring
Pawl Pin
Right Hand Ball Cup
Driver (3-Lug)
Driver Dust Cap
Cone
Locknut
Ball Retainer
Cone Lockwasher
Ball Cup Dust Cup
Loose Balls (20)
Pawl Spring
Spring Cap
Planet Gear Pin
Planet Gear
Early Model Thrust Ring
Axle Key
Clutch Spring
Thrust Washer
Clutch
Clutch Sleeve
Pawl Spring
Sun Gear Dowel Pin
Sun Gear
Axle
Pawl Pin
Planet Cage
Low Gear Pawl
Oil Cap
Ball Retainer
Cone
Cone Lockwasher
Locknut
Spacer Washer
Ball Cup Dust Cap
Hub Shell Assembly

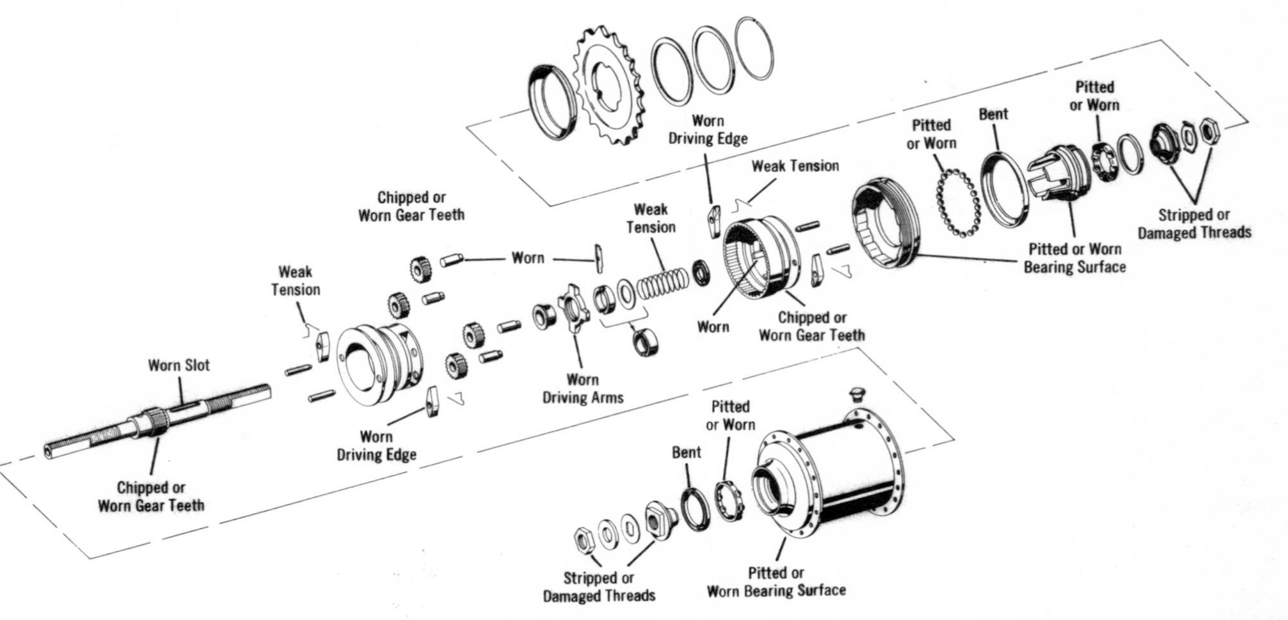

Exploded view of a Sturmey-Archer AW three-speed rear hub. (Schwinn Bicycle Company)

MAINTENANCE OF STURMEY-ARCHER HUBS

If gear changing is not smooth, first check to be certain that the indicator is even with the axle when the shifter is in the "normal" range (as described above).

Oil the hub through the opening in the hub shell, using only a good bicycle oil. Add a few drops of oil every one hundred miles or so.

Smoother cable action will result if you occasionally put a few drops of oil into the cable housing at the handlebar control end. To expose the opening, put the trigger or twist-grip control in the high position and unscrew the metal ferrule next to the control device. If your bicycle is equipped with the trigger control, an occasional oiling of the control unit will assure easy action.

If the hub becomes noisy or grinds even though all adjustments are correct, stop operation of the bike and carry the whole works to a bike shop. As you can see from the diagrams, this just isn't worth getting involved with.

SHIMANO 3·3·3 HUBS

A twist-grip shifter is furnished on all adult bikes with this hub. The grip will be marked L (low), N (normal or intermediate), and H (high).

A pivoted crank arm or lever is used to link the cable to the inside hub parts. Adjusting the shift is simple.

Set the twist grip (or, in a few junior models, the trigger) to N.

If the arrow on the hub does not point to the vertical line on the cap nut, release the lock nut on the cable and rotate the knurled joint until the arrow points correctly.

Then tighten the lock nut.

LOOSE WHEEL

If the rear axle nuts are tight but the wheel is loose or wobbly, the wheel should be tightened by adjusting the *right-*

hand cone on the sprocket side (*opposite* from the Sturmey-Archer hub).

Oil the Shimano hub through the opening in the hub shell, using a good bike oil. Add a few drops every one hundred miles or so.

OTHER MODELS

Other three-speed and five-speed hubs will be very similar in operation and adjustment to the two types listed here. Look for the indicator mark somewhere on the cap nut or the axle, then adjust to that mark with the gearshift in the mid-range position.

DÉRAILLEUR GEARS

This is a French word (Americanized to "de-railer," which is what it does) for the shifting devices that move the chain from one sprocket to another on five-, ten-, and fifteen-speed models. So instead of stopping to change sprockets to a better gear combination for road conditions, we have bicycles that carry five available sprockets on the rear wheel, and one, two, or three sprockets (five-, ten-, or fifteen-speed models) at the pedals, and we merely move the chain to the ones we want by moving levers.

As we shift, the chain is guided by the dérailleur to the selected sprocket combination, smaller in the rear and larger in the front for higher speeds on level roads or downhill, and the opposite for hill climbing or rough riding.

Eighty per cent of all bikes built in America are equipped with either the Huret Allvit (French), the Shimano (Japanese), or the "Schwinn Approved" model (built to this company's specs by whoever gets the job). We will concentrate on these models here. Similar in operation and maintenance, but considered to be higher on the quality list and used more for professional and racing applications, are the Simplex Prestige and the top-of-the-line (according to some) Campagnolo, made in Italy.

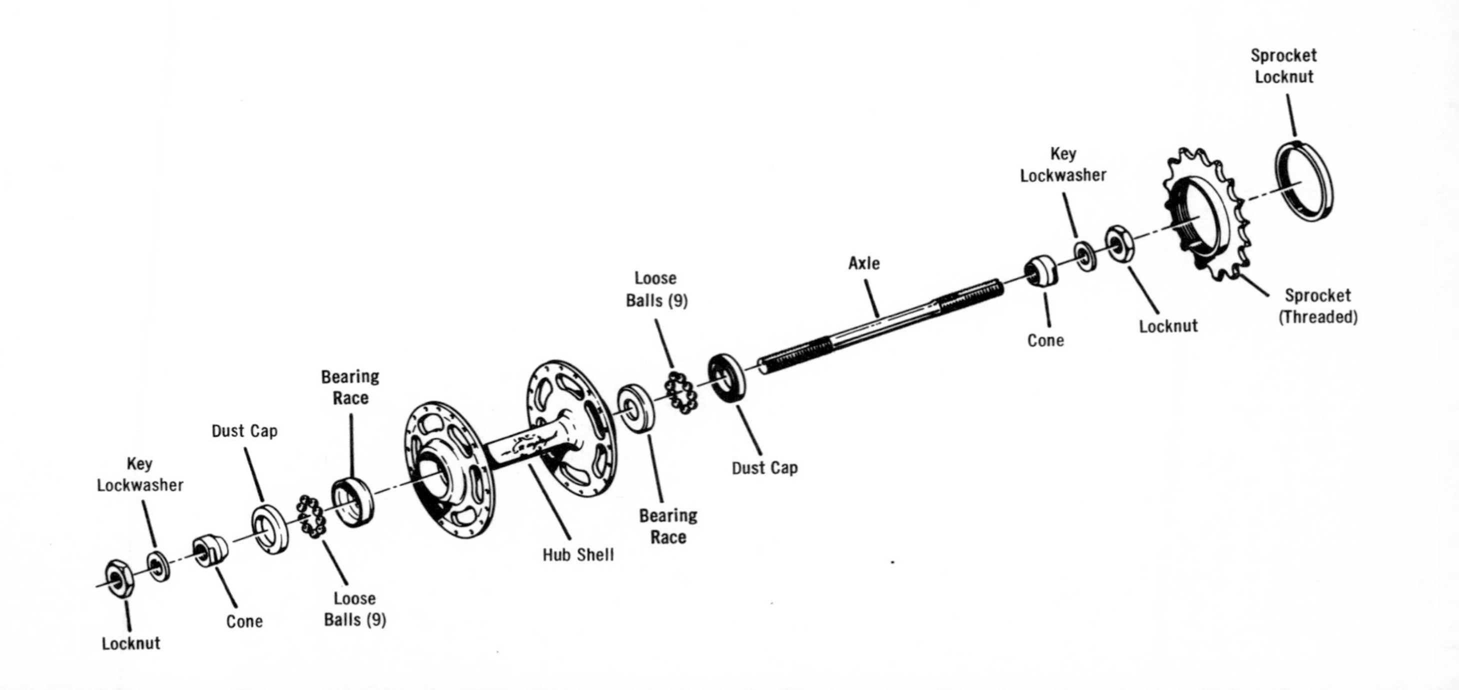
Sprocket Locknut
Sprocket (Threaded)
Locknut
Key Lockwasher
Cone
Axle
Dust Cap
Loose Balls (9)
Bearing Race
Hub Shell
Bearing Race
Loose Balls (9)
Dust Cap
Cone
Key Lockwasher
Locknut

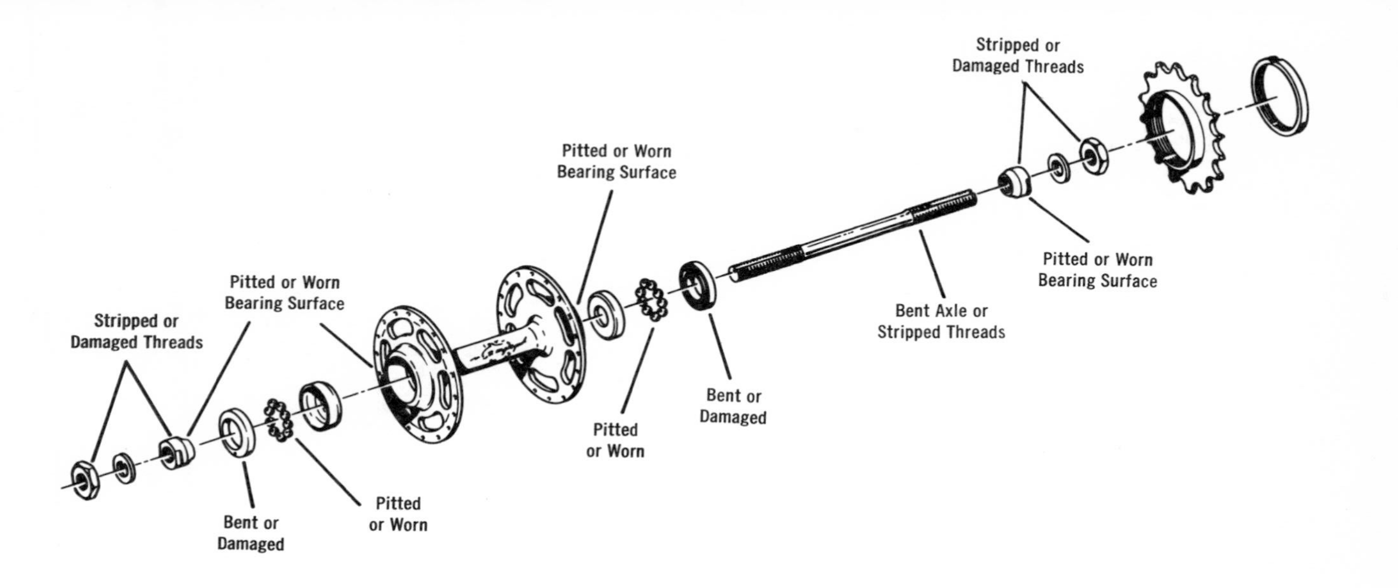

Exploded view of a typical fixed rear hub. (Schwinn Bicycle Company)

GEAR RATIO

Although some are smoother and quieter than others in operation, the actual make of the dérailleur might not be quite as important to pleasure riders as the *gear ratio.* A mild change in the number of teeth in the lower gears can make a solid difference halfway up a steep hill, especially for riders in average physical condition.

And here, too much quality can get you into difficulty, since the very best (and most expensive) bikes are generally set up for the most well-conditioned rider. The gears cover a rather narrow band of ratios, much like the close-ratio gearbox in a sports car.

If you are not in the best of condition, a lower low will be a great help, and generally the low lows are found in the wide-ratio gearing of the less expensive bikes.

If you want wide-ratio gearing, count the teeth on each of the gears or sprockets in the sprocket cluster, known as the freewheel, on the rear of the bike in question. You might get something like 14, 16, 18, 21, and 24 teeth, or maybe 13, 15, 17, 19, and 21 teeth. These are close-ratio gear clusters.

Ask the dealer to substitute the gear cluster with something like 15, 19, 21, 24, and 28. With either a single or a double chain wheel up front, you can see that you'll have a much wider selection from low to high gear.

MAKE THE GEARS WORK FOR YOU

Most serious cyclists consider a dérailleur a "must" under all riding conditions except on an enclosed track, and certainly regular hobby riders must now be considered almost as serious as the pros when bicycle riding is considered. The dérailleur system requires less energy to propel the bicycle than does the internally geared three- or five-speed hub; that is, a certain amount of the rider's energy goes into just operating the system itself, but less of it goes into the dérailleur system.

Using the dérailleur is simple. The rule is, always shift when

(The Huffman Company)

the pedals are in forward motion (opposite of the three-speed hubs), but without great pedaling force. The chain can be derailed from one sprocket to another only while it is moving forward, and the smoothest and quietest shift can be made with reduced pedaling power. When the bicycle is climbing a hill, for example, the shift should be made before you have slowed, so that the reduced pedaling power necessary for a smooth shift will not cost you forward speed. *Never force a shift*. Let the dérailleur do its work properly and it will take much of the effort out of riding.

Many riders, according to Schwinn experts, use higher gears than they should, resulting in excessive fatigue. The top, or "high" gears are best for riding downhill or with the wind at your back. Do most of your riding on level in the intermediate gears, as the experts do. *From fifty-five to eighty-five rpm of the pedals is considered the most efficient usage of body power.* It will improve your cycling technique if you occasionally shift to a low gear and "wind her up" to as much as 120 rpm.

ADJUSTMENT OF THE SHIMANO REAR DÉRAILLEUR

(To adjust this or any dérailleur, you must raise the rear wheel off the ground so the pedals can turn the wheel while adjustments are being made. A pair of pliers and a 5/16″ (or adjustable) wrench are needed. You may wish to turn the bike upside down. If the dérailleur is bent or broken, or if you are not accustomed to working on mechanical equipment, do not proceed with these adjustments and trouble-shooting methods. Take your bike to a qualified repairman.)

Chain Jumps off Smallest Gear

If the shifter is in high gear and the chain shifts too far out and runs off the small high gear, turn stop screw A to the right, or in. Turn the pedals, and test shift several times to be certain the adjustment is correct.

Chain Jumps off Largest Gear

If the shifter is in low gear and the chain shifts too far in and runs off the large low gear, turn stop screw B to the right, or in. Test shift several times.

Chain Does Not Move onto Smallest Gear

If the shifter is in high gear and the chain will not shift out to the smallest gear, turn stop screw A to the left, or out. Test shift.

If the dérailleur does not move out far enough with stop

screw A adjusted out, a cable adjustment is necessary to pull it farther. Loosen lock nut C and turn adjusting screw D to the left, or out. After the desired shifting is attained, tighten lock nut C. Now set stop screw A as above. If the adjusting screw will not take up enough cable, then the cable must be reset as explained below.

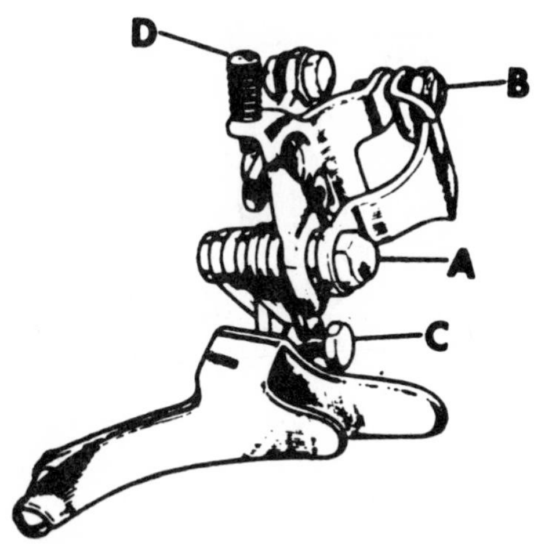

(The Huffman Company)

Chain Does Not Move onto Largest Gear

If the shifter is in low gear and the chain will not shift into the largest gear, turn stop screw B to the left, or out. Test shift.

If the dérailleur does not move in far enough with stop screw B adjusted out, a cable adjustment is necessary to pull it farther. Loosen lock nut E and turn adjusting screw F to the left, or out. After the desired shifting is attained, tighten lock nut E. Now set stop screw B as above. If the adjusting screw will not take up enough cable, then the cable must be reset as explained below.

Resetting the Cable

Set the shifter control so that it is centered between high and low.

Loosen cable clamp screws G.

While turning the pedals, push dérailleur by hand into position behind the middle gear so that chain has shifted to this gear and runs quietly.

Turn both adjusting screws D and F all the way down (for later adjustment). See that both cables are outside the screws G and under the clamps H.

Pull one cable snug but not hard enough to move the shifter, and then hold it tight while tightening screw G securely. Check to see that the shifter is still centered.

Pull the other cable tight, and secure the other screw G.

Test shift and, if necessary, make adjustments listed above.

ADJUSTMENT OF FRONT DÉRAILLEUR

The chain cage must be perfectly in line with the front chain wheel. If necessary, loosen the frame clamp nuts A and B, align, and then retighten the nuts.

Place the left control lever forward, loosen lock nut C, and move the derailing cage laterally (sideways) to center it over the smaller chain wheel; then tighten the lock nut. The curvature of the cage must be kept parallel to the chain wheel.

Place the left control lever back and adjust lateral movement by screw D so that the cage is centered over the larger chain wheel.

Be certain these adjustments are made so that the chain cannot be derailed to the left of the inside chain wheel or to the right of the outside chain wheel.

ADJUSTMENT OF THE FRONT AND REAR HURET AND "SCHWINN APPROVED" DÉRAILLEURS

Check alignment of the dérailleur rollers with the rear sprocket. If rollers are not parallel with the rear sprockets,

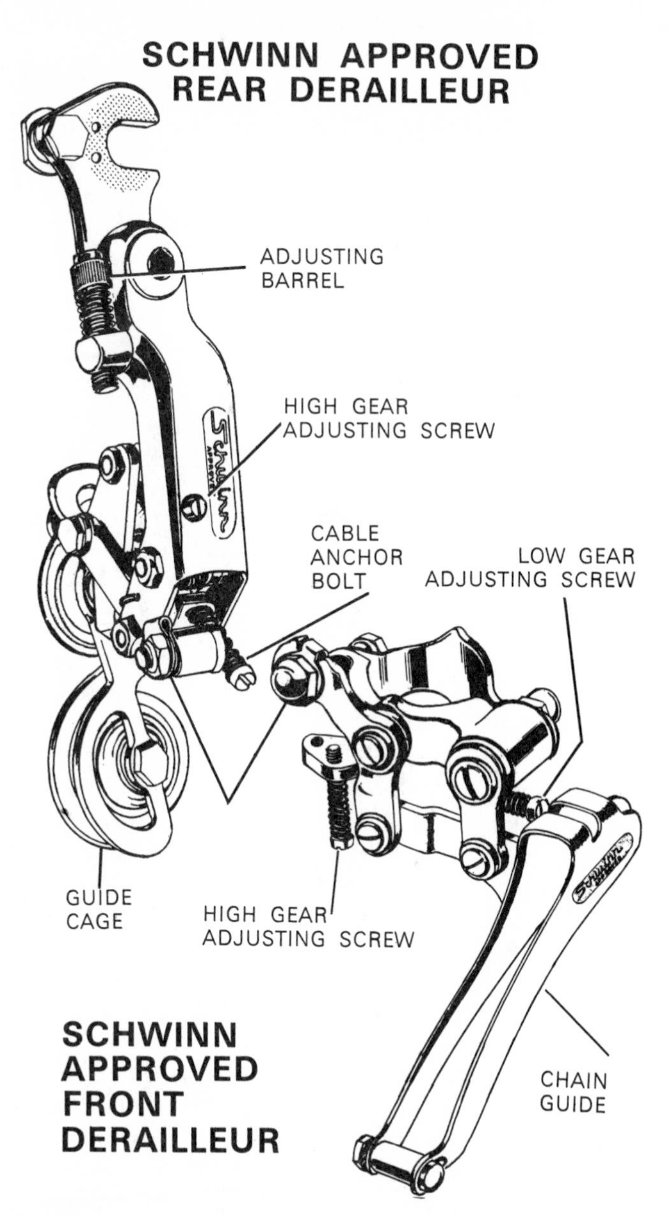

(Schwinn Bicycle Company)

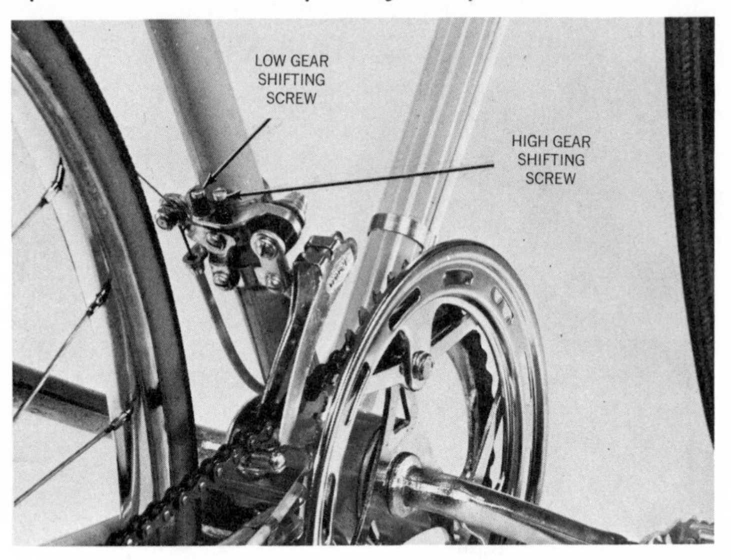

(The Huffman Company)

use an adjustable wrench to gently twist the dérailleur back into position.

Should either the front or the rear dérailleur shift by itself while you are riding, tighten the thumbscrew holding the shifting lever at the stem. Do not tighten too much, or shifting will be difficult.

If the cable has stretched and the rear dérailleur will not shift into low gear, shift unit to high gear by turning the pedals and pushing the shifting lever all the way forward. Turn the adjusting barrel until the cable is *almost* tight. If there is no adjustment left on the adjusting barrel, turn the adjusting barrel as far down as possible, then loosen the cable anchor bolt nut and pull the cable through until it is *almost* taut. Retighten the cable anchor bolt nut. Fine adjustment can now be made with the adjusting barrel, explained above.

If the front dérailleur does not shift to high gear, push the left lever all the way forward while turning the pedals. Loosen the cable anchor bolt nut and pull the cable through until it is *almost* taut. Retighten the cable anchor bolt nut.

After a period of time it may be necessary to readjust the entire dérailleur system. If seeing a Schwinn dealer is inconvenient, primary adjustments can be made as follows:

Shift front dérailleur onto the small front sprocket. Turn the low-gear shifting screw until the chain guide is centered over the sprocket. In this position the lever should be all the way forward and the cable should be *almost* taut.

Shift the chain onto the large front sprocket. Turn the high-gear adjusting screw until the chain guide is centered over the sprocket.

Shift the chain onto the smallest rear sprocket. If the cable is not almost taut, readjust the cable, following the stretched-cable instructions above. If the guide cage is not centered over the chain and sprocket, turn the high-gear adjusting screw as needed.

Shift the chain onto the largest rear sprocket. If the guide cage is not centered over the chain and sprocket, turn the low-gear adjusting screw as needed.

FRONT AND REAR SHIFTING-CONTROL LEVERS

As noted previously, these levers control the spring-loaded dérailleurs and depend on friction to hold them where they are set. With use, they may loosen. They can be tightened by turning the thumb or wing nuts that hold them.

GEAR CONVERSION

There are hub gear-conversion units, such as the Benelux, for coverting Sturmey-Archer AW and SW three-speed gears into nine-speed units. Available from specialty bicycle shops and suppliers, this kit provides the nine speeds by the addition of a three-sprocket gear set and a dérailleur to the standard three-speed hub. Three in the hub times three at the sprockets equals nine separate speeds. Cost is less than fifteen dollars.

6

Wheels and Tires

The wheel of a bicycle is made up of axle, hub, spokes, a rim, a tube, and a tire. If your wheel is loose, if you can move it from side to side on its axle, refer to the HUB section of this chapter. If your wheel wobbles back and forth as it is turning, go to the SPOKES section. If your tire is flat, to the TIRES section with you.

RIM

Aluminum-alloy rims are the best. They are lighter than and almost as strong as steel, which is cheaper but heavier. Rims are also made of other alloys. Some are solid, and some are tubular. All are fragile.

If your bike has hand brakes, it is important to keep the rim reasonably clean and rust free, since the side of the rim is one of the braking surfaces. Not only does a clean rim look better, and stop you faster, but a dirty rim can drastically wear down brake pads quickly.

Dings on a rim should be removed, if for no other reason than braking efficiency. This is a job that can sometimes be accomplished with a set of visegrips, applied *lovingly*.

HUB

The hub of a bicycle wheel is made up of an axle, two bearing sets, and the casing, which you see at the center of your wheel and inside which the axle turns on the bearings. Again, aluminum seems to be the preference of expert riders, though steel and other alloys will do the job just about as well.

If your wheel seems loose on the axle and can be wiggled from side to side, you must correct this problem before you ride again. If you don't, you risk flattening or even breaking your bearings.

First be certain that this looseness is not just a wheel loose in the frame. Check the nuts that hold the wheel in the drop outs, and tighten them if they are loose. This might correct the problem.

If the wheel is actually loose on the axle, loosen the left axle nut; then, with a thin wrench, tighten the left bearing cone until it is snug. Back it off one half turn, and then retighten the big axle nut. The wheel should spin freely, but it should no longer wiggle if everything has seated properly and the bearings are not shot.

Three or four drops of oil into each bearing will help to keep things running smoothly.

SPOKES

Spokes are the wires that go between the hub and the rim and hold the wheel round. Individually they are springy and weak-appearing, but installed and tightened correctly they are quite strong.

But not so strong that they cannot be broken or bent or twisted out of shape if you go around colliding with hard things.

Spokes are held in holes in the flanges on each side of the hub. At the rim end they are screwed into nipples that fit through holes in the rim. There are steel spokes, piano-wire spokes, stainless-steel spokes, chrome spokes, and even butted ones (thicker at the ends, where the need is greatest, and thinner in the middle, where strength is not quite so important, for weight reduction).

All the spokes on a particular wheel should be the same type and size, so if you must replace spokes, take an original in and match it exactly. All the spokes in a wheel should be of uniform tension, so first of all you might go around the wheel with a spoke wrench and be sure they are all firm.

FOR A WHEEL WOBBLE

Adjusting spokes is a tricky job. You can adjust out one big wobble and wind up with four little ones, or vice versa. You might get rid of a wobble, and then find it has just moved to the other side of the wheel. If you really want the easy way, take the wheel to a shop and have a professional true it, but if you can stand a little vexation and have a solid supply of patience, you can try it yourself.

First of all, you need a reference point. If you have hand brakes, adjust them until they just barely brush the rim at the point of the wobble. This tells you exactly where the problem is as the wheel turns. If you do not have hand brakes or some other convenient reference point, you might loosen the big axle nuts and twist the wheel until it is "cocked" in the frame, until it just brushes the frame at the point of greatest wobble.

You're ready to begin, so deflate the tire, take a deep breath, and plan to take your time. Try to think of the wobble as a *group* of misbehaving spokes and not just one, single offensive spoke. So go to the bad group and check them against the rest of the spokes. Are they looser? Tighter? Or what? If you see no difference at the point of wobble, then begin precise adjustment.

If you wish to move the rim to the *left*, you will want to *tighten* the spokes that go to the *left* side of the hub and loosen the spokes that go to the right side of the hub. *Left, tighten left.* Tighten, and loosen, a little at a time, checking constantly, and working with a group of eight or ten spokes in the area of the wobble.

So that you won't just move the one big wobble out to each

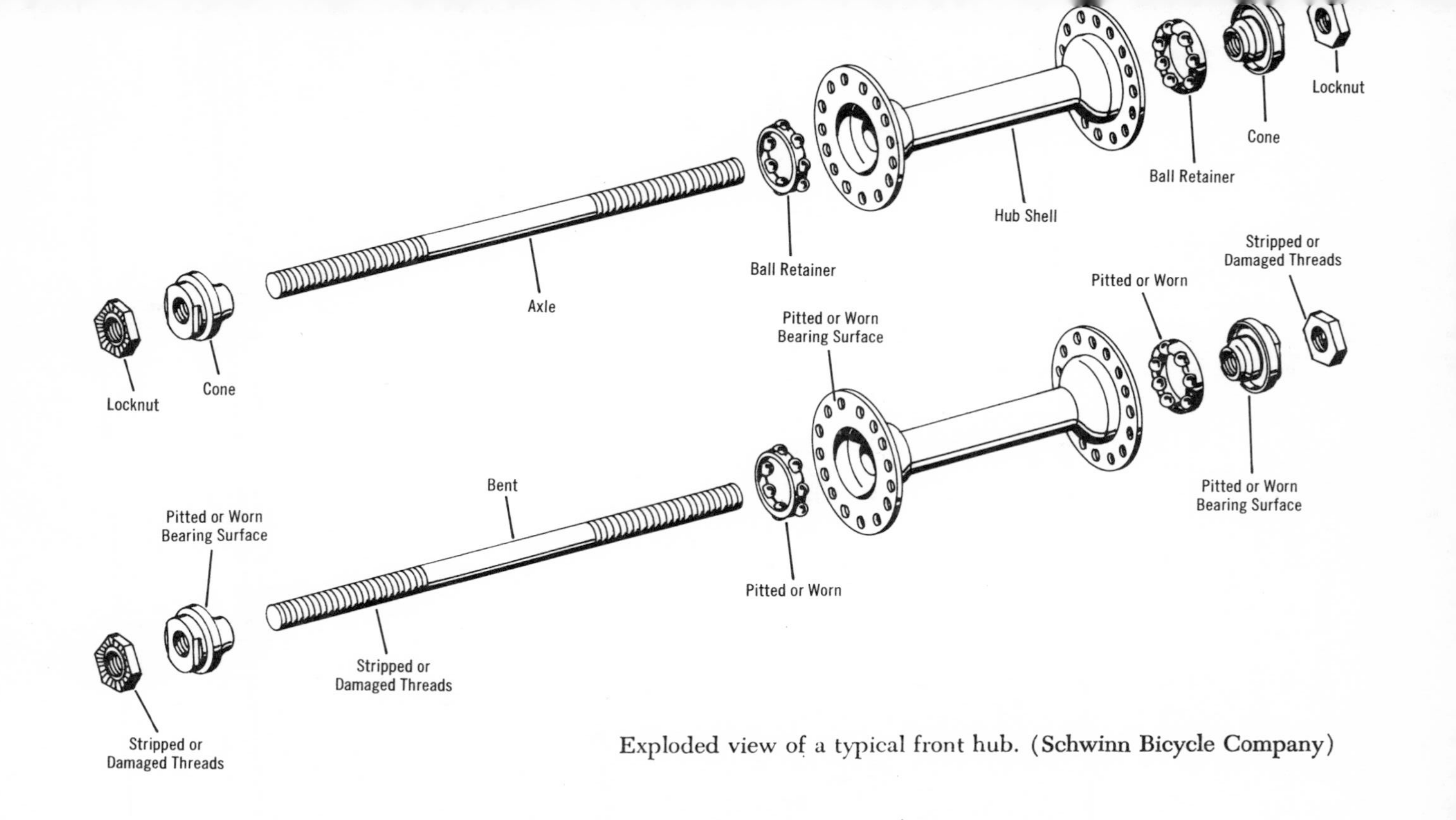

Exploded view of a typical front hub. (Schwinn Bicycle Company)

end and form two little wobbles, make greater changes in the center of the wobble and more minor changes in spoke tension near the edges.

Leave no spokes completely loose. Remember, each spoke should have the same tension (though, in practice, this might not be exactly the case).

On a ten-speed rear wheel the rim is "dished" on the side where the freewheel sprocket cluster is located. Look straight down at the wheel from above, and you will see that the spokes go out farther on the left side. This is often accomplished by merely tightening the spokes to a greater tension on the right side, pulling the rim to the right. In this case, the tension difference will be obvious (count the threads showing at the nipple on each side, just so you understand why).

On front wheels, again, the tension should be nearly the same on all spokes.

Whenever you replace bent or broken spokes, use spokes of exactly the same length and thickness, and remember that the indentation, the countersink, in the hub flange is not for the *head* of the spoke, but for the *curve* at the head end.

Before you reinflate the tire, run your finger all the way around the rim under the protective rubber rim strip to be sure there are no spoke tips poking up where they might punch through the strip and puncture the tube. If you find any, remove the tire and tube; then file them down flat.

TIRES

There are two basic types of bicycle tires: clinchers (with a rim bead and a tube like the family car tires) and tubulars (the type they sew up around the tube).

TUBULARS

Tubulars, the least common type, are very light in weight, with a very lightweight inner tube completely enclosed in a stitched-up casing. They are more prone to flats, and difficult to repair if they do flatten, but with their lightweight characteristics and rims they are very responsive, and preferred by professional riders. A plus for tubulars is that where they are very difficult to repair, they are much easier to replace, and a spare is very easy to carry along strapped under the seat or on the top tube.

CLINCHERS

Clinchers have a U-shaped cross section just like the tires we know, and they are much more popular than tubulars. They have a separate inner tube, and since they are heavier and stronger, they are more resistant to flats and other damage. Repairs are easy, and this type is less expensive to buy in the first place.

Since clinchers are found on the majority of bikes purchased in this country for other than professional use, let's leave the tubulars to the racers and study the clinchers.

PROPER INFLATION

More money, after purchase price of your bike is considered, is spent on tires and tire repairs and tire replacement than any other single bicycle item. And most of this is due to tire neglect, especially where proper inflation is concerned. So, since improper inflation can cost you more than anything else, see that it doesn't happen and you will save a good deal of money.

Remember that it is perfectly normal for a tube to gradually lose air due to the porosity of rubber. *It is important that proper inflation be checked and maintained.* With your bicycle will have come a tire chart, or any bike shop can give you such a chart, or the information will be imprinted on the side of the tire, but wherever you find it, know the proper inflation figure. As a rule of thumb, for the new lightweight bike tires, the tire should feel firm, almost hard, between the thumb and forefinger. The shape of the tire should change very little when you mount and dismount. You might try checking your own "feel" against a good tire gauge until you become familiar with exactly how they should look and feel with the proper amount of air.

Also remember that service-station air pumps can emit a very large *volume* of air at a very high pressure. Your tires, where they may need a relatively high pressure, will not hold much volume, so be very careful at the local gas-station pumps. In only a few seconds a tire can be inflated and blown out. A hand pump is best.

Never sit on your bike, or ride, with underinflated tires. You will certainly damage the tire and the tube, and you might even damage the rim. Top riders won't even *push* their bikes to an air supply on an underinflated tire. They *carry* the machine.

TIRE AND TUBE DAMAGE

Tires and tubes can suffer damage for a variety of reasons that have nothing to do with inflation or lack of it. *Ruptures* in the tire, caused by running over objects such as curbs, sharp stones, and potholes, are only one problem. Others are *rim bruises,* in which the tire is crushed between the rim and an object; *rim cuts,* caused by rusty rims and overloading; *chafing,* caused by crooked wheels, improper alignment of the wheel in the frame, bent fork, or improperly positioned accessory rollers that touch the tire wrong; *broken beads,* generally caused by improper use of tools (always use your hands when mounting or dismounting bicycle tires); and *general cuts and bruises* caused by hitting objects on the road.

Distorted tire casings can be the result of long storage with the bike standing on its wheels. If you're going to pack your bike away, say for the winter, either turn it upside down or, better yet, hang it from hooks or a rack on the garage wall. Most bicycle stores carry huge hooks that have been padded with plastic for this purpose.

FLAT TIRE OR BLOWOUT

Just to be sure (in the case of a flat, not a blowout, which is obvious), check the tire valve first. With at least some air in the tire, spit on your finger and wipe it across the valve end. If bubbles appear, the stem is probably loose and you have saved yourself a half-hour job. Tighten or replace the stem and inflate the tire. If that isn't the problem:

Remove the wheel from the bike.

Remove the tire from the wheel. Grasp the tire on both sides and press down toward the floor. This will force one bead up away from the rim, and with a bit more hand pressure, down over the rim. Work your way around the wheel in this manner until one bead is outside the rim. If you *must* use a tool, on a very tight tire, use only a rounded tire iron (not a screwdriver), and be certain that you are not pinching the tube against the rim, for you could wind up with two holes or more.

Pull the tube out, and if the leak isn't obvious (the nail may still be in the tire, so there would be no doubt), inflate the tube and locate the leak. If the tube goes down as fast as you inflate it, replace the tube rather than patch it. If the leak is a tiny one, patching should do the job.

Mark the location of the leak on the *tire,* so that you can be certain that whatever caused the leak is not still present.

Deflate the tube and patch it with a good tire-patching kit. Be certain the area of the patch is clean and roughed up with the cap of the kit can. Don't touch the sticky side of the patch. When the repair is complete, dust a bit of talcum powder over the patch so that the glue won't stick to the inner surface of the tire.

Examine the tire casing carefully before reinserting the tube. Make sure it is clean and free from breaks or other tube-injuring conditions.

Examine the rim carefully. It must not be bent, and it must be free from dirt and rust. Be sure there are no loose or protruding spoke ends visible.

Always use the rim strip, and be certain the strip covers all spoke heads.

Inflate the tube with about ten pounds of air after you have replaced it and reinstalled the tire (using your hands) on the rim. Be certain the tire is on the rim correctly; then deflate the tire. Inflate it to its proper pressure for the final time.

Replace the wheel on the bike.

7

Accessories

Many experienced riders agree with architect Mies van der Rohe, who said "less is more." Accessories, they snort, are for children's balloon-tired bombers. To carry this point to its logical conclusion, the well-known $330 Bob Jackson track bike, built in England, weighs but fourteen and one half pounds. It has one gear, and nothing else except the absolutely necessary wheels, frame, seat, and handlebar. It doesn't even have *brakes* (nor do any other pure racing bikes, since the idea is to *go,* not to stop.).

But let's be reasonable on this accessory point. And let us not get into the aesthetics of the lightweight models currently available, stripped for action and ready for the high road. There are young teen-agers who with all honesty feel that their chopped and channeled, twin-stick, mag-equipped, slick-tired drag special with banana seat and sissy bar is the most beautiful thing God ever put on earth, including Yosemite National Park. All it lacks, they tell their parents, are a speedometer, twin tail lights with directional signals, and a wood-grain console. Maybe later a radio and twin rear-view mirrors.

Don't laugh. Every one of these items is available.

And so are brake-lever extensions, raccoon tails, handgrip

streamers, imitation-zebra-skin seat covers, and chromed exhaust heads.

Just the *reading* of these last paragraphs is enough to make the purist turn purple.

And yet, certain accessories (admit it now, you purists) are efficient, comfortable . . . and necessary.

Take a bike lock for example. Day by day, we are not becoming noted for our increasing honesty, and bikes have now replaced surfboards, on the West Coast at least, as the single most stolen item. One boy had his bicycle stolen from his front patio in Southern California. So he took to bringing the new one in and keeping it in his bedroom. It was stolen from there, finally.

The city fathers of one small western town provided an initial ten bicycles after the Police Department reported that the bicycle theft problem would be relieved if courtesy bikes were available. By placing bright yellow "city" bikes at various locations to meet the transportation needs of questionably honest youngsters, it was felt that a potential thief would just borrow instead.

In short order all that was left not stolen was a few broken frames, wheels with kicked-out spokes, and slashed tires. Wholesale theft and vandalism halted the program quickly. Why? Who knows? Protect your bike.

Use a good, strong, stainless-steel chain and lock. Not a cheap one, but an expensive one. One that defies the jaws of the best cutters. Don't padlock a one-hundred-dollar bike with a one-dollar lock.

Lock your bike every single time you leave it, even for a minute. Run the chain around the frame, through a wheel, and then around a stationary object that cannot be moved.

Meanwhile, have the serial number of your bike on record at home, and with the police department if your town has a bicycle license system. True, these recording systems are of questionable good (the Los Angeles Police Department recently admitted that though bicycles are one of the most stolen items, the recovery rate is only 14 per cent, but, then, every little bit helps, and some bicycle thieves avoid bikes with licenses on them).

A good lock is the best answer, so let's just add that accessory to the basic bike. But what else? There must be at least fifty pounds of junk available for hanging on a poor bicycle frame.

Decide, yourself, how you plan to use the bicycle. If accessories weren't popular and selling, the latest catalogues from major manufacturers wouldn't have several pages of them listed. Somebody out there is buying them, and using them, and the kids just don't have that much money.

It could be a situation similar to automobiles. Some of us prefer "loaded" Cadillacs, and others only love stripped-down sports cars. So what do you want?

You have to stand the bike when you leave it. Kickstands are available, though many bikes now have this item as standard equipment.

Add a basket or a carrying rack if you plan to carry things on your bike. Why shouldn't a student, even if he owns a sleek, ten-speed, semi-racing model, have a place to strap his books? Sure it's an extra, added item, but it makes the bike much safer and more convenient to ride.

Lights? Troublesome extra weight, especially with a wheel-rubbing generator, and they do nothing but get in the way all day long. But, then again, at night they are a darned handy item. So do you plan to ride at night? A horn? It could be a legal requirement in your state. So could lights be, for that matter.

Tailor your bike for your own needs. Not many riders need a speedometer, for instance, but if you do for some reason, then attach one. They aren't expensive, they don't weigh much, and they are accurate. And for rally riders, the odometer on modern speedometers is quite reliable.

If you plan to ride far from home base, you might consider strapping one of the new light tire pumps to your seat mast or down tube. Spare tubes, sure, if you plan to ride cross-country, far from any service facility. Include a small tool kit, which can be purchased as an accessory item and fits neatly under the seat. If you plan to bicycle around town, on the other hand, this extra weight and expense are not necessary.

Today's bikes, with the very wide variety of almost every possible accessory you can think of, can be custom fitted to suit each individual owner's needs.

So if you see a bike with a chromed exhaust head, don't laugh. The proud owner may have just as much personal reason for adding that attachment as you had for adding your basket, or speedometer, or helper wheels.

But *handlebar streamers . . .* ?

Nobody could find a good use for *them!*

8

Be a Bike Driver, Not Rider

Bounce these statistics around for just a moment before you go into the boring "safety lists" that follow. According to the Health Insurance Association, bicycle riding is bringing better health to millions of new riders, and prosperity to bicycle manufacturers, but many of us are going to get injured . . . or worse.

The next chapter in this book will show you how steady pedaling can keep you physically fit. Cycling is better than jogging, according to many doctors, and much less monotonous. You can keep in shape with three or four sessions a week, a half hour to an hour per session. At five miles per hour, you burn up 4.5 calories more *each minute* than sitting still.

The trouble is, an estimated 120,000 to 150,000 riders are expected to be injured in some way, or disabled, in the United States for as long as the bicycle boom lasts. Each year of the boom, it is predicted that as many as 750 persons will lose their lives in bicycle mishaps.

Studies show that the peak rate of bicycling deaths occurs among riders of ages ten to fourteen. The second highest rate is at ages five to nine. If you reach twenty years of age and are a bicycle rider, your chances of being injured drop sharply. But your chances of being hurt rise again when you reach sixty-four years of age.

In an effort to convince younger riders that when a bike and a car come together the bike usually loses, they have a "talking" bicycle in Wabash, Indiana. With a grand entrance of sirens screaming, and a policeman as a rider (often "pulling over" the school principal on another bike), "Mike the Bike" talks safety to the kids. And Mike makes sense to listening adults as well.

With the help of Schwinn, which built the bike, Honeywell, which built the electronics, and several other firms, which donated parts, Mike is directed by Wabash Police Department policemen. And no matter what we purists might think, when a racy, yellow three-speed with red lights and sirens does the talking, young riders *listen.*

Fort Wayne, Indiana, also has a talking bicycle, and other cities are considering adding a "Mike" to their safety staffs. These bikes lay it on the line, either as a lecture spiced with humor or as a question-and-answer session with a policeman who knows what to ask. They go over the fact that bikes are ruled by the same laws as cars, and that bike citations in larger cities, such as Los Angeles, for example, are commonplace. Most citations, explains the bicycle, are for riding on the wrong side of the road, for no lights, for failure to give the right of way to pedestrians, and for failure to stop at a stop sign.

"People get run over by bikes, you know," explains the bike.

Chatty Mike gives advice on parking, and handling of a bicycle around pedestrians. He insists that you not leave your bike in a driveway or a street.

"Have you ever seen a bicycle that has been run over by an automobile?" he asks with a catch in his voice. Then, after a pause, he answers himself glumly: "My, what a *sickening* sight!"

YOUR BIKE MUST "FIT"

To be safe, and efficient, your bike must "fit" you properly. That's why bicycles come in several sizes and, as an option for considerably extra, they can be custom-built to your personal measurements.

Your bike uses almost every single one of the muscles you have, so proper fit to your whole body is very important. If your bike does not fit, you will be uncomfortable and easily fatigued, and your control will not be as good as it could be. You will even wear painful blisters here and there, mostly there . . . and you know where *that* is.

The frame size of your bike should allow you to straddle the horizontal top bar and stand flat-footed in stockinged feet on the ground.

The saddle position is next. Too low a saddle causes extra fatigue and discomfort, and too high a saddle prevents effective use of your leg muscles.

Remember: Set the nose of the saddle about two inches behind an imaginary line drawn vertically through the center of the bottom bracket. Then, with the pedal in the lowest position, raise the saddle until the heel (again in stockinged feet) just rests on the pedal, with the leg straight, when seated in a natural position on the saddle. When the ball of the foot is placed on the pedal in proper pedaling position, the knee should have a very slight bend.

SAFETY RULES

The list of rules isn't really so bad. Reading time is only one minute.

Observe All Traffic Regulations

Bicycle riding is governed by traffic regulations similar to those for automobile driving. If ever in doubt, follow the automobile laws.

Keep to the Right

Ride in a straight line, single file, close to the right-hand curb or the right side of the road. Be alert for parked cars pulling out into traffic and for car doors being opened suddenly in your path.

Give Pedestrians the Right of Way

Avoid sidewalks, unless local ordinances permit sidewalk riding. Allow plenty of room when approaching pedestrians, and avoid startling them.

Always Use Proper Hand Signals

Signals are very important to those behind you, so use your arm when you are planning to stop, or to turn right or left.

Slow Down at All Intersections

Then look to the right and to the left before crossing.

Keep Both Hands on the Handlebar

Except when signaling, both hands should be on the handlebar for best control. It's foolish and dangerous to ride "Look, Ma, no hands!"

Do Not Carry Packages Dangerously

Packages in the hands, or under the arms, might obstruct your vision, and they certainly hurt your control of the bicycle. There are carriers and baskets available as optional accessories, which carry items safely and efficiently without interfering with the bike's operation.

Have a White Light on the Front and a Reflector on the Rear

For any night riding, you must be visible. Lights can be battery powered or generator powered.

Have a Signal Device

Bells and horns are available as optional accessories to warn of your approach.

Be Sure Your Brakes Are Operating Efficiently

Stopping safely is of greatest importance.

Never "Hitch" a Ride on Another Vehicle

And don't stunt, or race, in traffic.

Never Carry Other Riders.

It is dangerous and in some states illegal, unless your bicycle was designed for two or is equipped with a solid child's seat.

YOUR FIRST RIDE ON A LIGHTWEIGHT

The lightweight bicycle is much more responsive and sensitive than the heavier bikes we first became accustomed to riding. So you may notice a tendency to overcontrol the first time out. You might tend to wobble. Anticipate this, and you will quickly conquer it.

Don't attempt to shift gears the first half block. First get a solid feel of the bike, a firm control whatever gear you're in, then try gently moving your hand to the shift lever and resting it there. Then move your hand back to the handlebar. Then back again to the shift lever. When you can accomplish this movement on the sensitive lightweight bike without an undue amount of wobbling, you are ready to shift gears.

Shift from top to bottom, front sprockets and rear, one at a time, then several gears at a time, until you get the "feel" of gear shifting, and until the positions of the levers become familiar. If properly done, a gearshift should make no more noise than a pleasant "thunk" as the chain sets on its new sprocket.

There will be no noticeable change in pedal speed when gears are shifted at the right time. But if you wait until a gear shift is absolutely necessary before making it, the change in foot speed will destroy your pedaling rhythm and increase fatigue.

Learn to use your gears as they were built to be used. Just because a hill is coming up ahead is no reason to shift to the lowest gear on the bike (unless you are riding on a three-speed). Select your gears for the job, moving from gear to gear. Use the flexibility that dérailleur gearing offers to get the best gear for each condition.

9

For Health and Riding Happiness

"There are four reasons I give for vigorous use of the leg muscles . . . not simply the arm muscles . . . and the first is physiological. We as bipeds need something to help us keep the blood circulating up from the lower part of our body."

So says eminent heart specialist Dr. Paul Dudley White in the Schwinn motion picture *Magic of the Bicycle.*

Dr. White continues:

"The leg muscles are very important. When they contract, they squeeze the veins (which have valves) and actually pump blood up toward the heart. This allows the heart to receive more blood with which to supply the brain.

"This is physiological and, therefore, we have proof that it isn't simply the heart that is the only pump. The leg muscles are pumps and the diaphragm is a suction pump. So by keeping fit, we help the heart in its action.

"Psychologically, too, exercise such as cycling . . . it could be walking or swimming but cycling is an especially favorable type of exercise . . . has a very good effect on the brain, on the mental state, and on the psyche. It's the best antidote . . . this kind of muscular exercise . . . for stress and mental fatigue. Instead of using tranquilizers, I advise muscular action . . . even to the point of fatigue, so that you won't need medicine to tranquilize you.

"We have a great problem today . . . and have had right along because we no longer use our legs properly . . . of being subject to thrombosis; that is, blood clotting in our leg veins. These blood clots can form and get established where there's too much stasis . . . sluggish circulation. This is a hazard . . . a great hazard . . . to life because blood clots can go from our leg veins to our lungs and kill us.

"The fourth reason . . . and perhaps the most important of all . . . is that there is clear evidence now that vigorous use of our muscles helps delay the onset of arteriosclerosis which is the modern epidemic in this country today.

"There are the four reasons I give for vigorous use of the leg muscles such as that performed best perhaps on bicycles."

What Dr. White is *not* saying, of course, is that we all rush out and buy bicycles, then pedal off on a twenty-mile ride over hill and dale. But overweight and poor general condition has been called America's number one health problem, and bicycling has proved to be a solid help.

And yet bicycling, even when you take it up as an exercise, is not hard work. Especially when you consider the amount of good it does your body. No grinding, repetitive, muscle-bending workouts here. No steam baths here or crash diets, but rather pleasant excursions you can look forward to, and do you just as much good.

You'll lose weight, and you'll tone up your body with proper riding—and you'll enjoy doing it. And with proper understanding of bike-riding principles, you can even increase your enjoyment of cycling. You can travel with less strain, and build up your average speed and distance, without tiring yourself.

RIDE AS THE EXPERTS RIDE

An experienced cyclist, one who has been riding for years and has learned all the tricks, will use only 40–50 per cent of the energy required by a beginner to cover the same distance. Think about that. A 50 per cent reduction of energy output means a rider could go twice as far before becoming fatigued.

How do the experts do this? By knowing and using certain efficient riding techniques and by using the lightweight's gearing possibilities to the best advantage. Once a rider has the hang of these bikes and has made the change from flab to at least a start toward physical conditioning, there are few hills he cannot conquer. The fascinating hobby of bicycle travel is ready and waiting.

The experienced rider does not "pedal" a bike with his legs to make it go. He uses the muscles in his entire body as a team. His legs, his arms, his back, each works without strain to propel the bicycle, each shares the load. He sits correctly, and he travels smoothly, at an even pace, without wavering and without moving his body about carelessly. With Maes-type drop handlebars, he is bent at an angle that, once accepted and made a habit, will be comfortable and efficient. With all-rounder bars he sits straighter but still with his body almost a part of the machine.

The real sign of an experienced bicyclist is the track he leaves. He will ride in a perfectly straight line, not wavering side to side more than an inch or two at any speed. Up a hill, he will shift without losing speed and without wavering from his straight line. Like an automobile racing driver, whose hands and feet move in concert to make the machine go forward at its best and most efficient speed, so moves an expert bicycle rider.

As a new rider, train yourself to ride in a straight line. You must apply pressure smoothly, "ankling" the pedals all around instead of just pressing them down. *Think* of them going around and around instead of up and down as you pedal. Train your body to respond to the bicycle, to become a part of the bicycle, and your riding enjoyment will quickly increase while your fatigue factor drops noticeably.

You will find yourself able to go much farther than before, with less effort involved. Many young cyclists who are looking at the sport more seriously than a simple ride to the corner store find that they can rather suddenly do far more with the bike than before. Much like swimmers who have swum for years but then decide they would like to *really* swim. So they think about it and concentrate on it. They *work* at it a bit. And suddenly everything seems to come together. They are *swimming*.

You can't even really say just when it happened, but as a swimmer or a bicyclist (or a participant in many other sports) your body just seems to begin to "work." This will be especially true if you began riding years ago on a balloon-tired coaster-brake model and are just now switching to a lightweight ten-speed. At first nothing seems to function the way it should, and you wiggle and wobble down the street, lurching every time you reach for what seem to you to be the most inconveniently placed shift levers possible.

Stay with it. It'll work just the way it's supposed to work when you get everything together. When your hands and feet and back and legs and wrists and head all begin to operate on the same frequency, you'll see that it all smooths out and riding becomes a pleasure.

WORKING UP TO IT

Meanwhile you can be building your own endurance. Remember that Dr. White did not say to jump on a bike and ride off into the hills. In fact, for a while at least, you'd better not ride off *anywhere* unless there is a bus coming back. If your total distance without collapse is four miles, remember that you can ride only to a destination two miles away (since you also must ride back again). It's even better if your two-mile destination is uphill from where you started, so that you can relax on the homeward journey. Work up to distances, as explained later in this chapter.

This could be amusing to many readers who have been cyclists for years and who are totally confident of their ability to get home from where they have pedaled, but you take a thirty-five-year-old office worker who has ridden the subway to his desk since hiring day, and you'll find a person who thinks his endurance is about ten times what it really is on a bicycle.

Cycling is great fun, and excellent for health, but let's not overdo it the first day out.

DRESS PROPERLY

Clothing can be important to riding comfort and efficiency. You'll rapidly warm up riding a bike, so take that into account and wear lightweight, non-bulky clothing that won't catch the wind or interfere with the smooth motion of the body.

Reduce the weight of your feet with lightweight, comfortable shoes that will not restrict foot action.

Of course if you are planning to ride into the teeth of a blizzard, which is a questionable idea in the first place, you'll want to wear warmer clothing and warmer shoes, but even then you might cheat a bit. Wear a wool sweater with a nylon windbreaker and perhaps lined mittens with cuffs to keep the icy blasts from going up your arms. You might consider wearing the same type of lightweight shoes, but a size or so larger so that you can wear extra pairs of warm socks (instead of heavy shoes).

LOSING WEIGHT, A SPECIFIC WORD

We've all heard the arguments. Why should I exercise? I can "sweat off" weight for an hour in a steam bath or by work, and one simple drink of water, which my body needs, puts it all back on again.

Or, I would have to run around the block several times to burn off the calories in one simple extra treat. It just isn't worth it.

The better way, these exercise haters insist, is to merely watch your intake in the first place. True, of course. Diet is important for weight watching or reducing.

But so is exercise, and don't let anybody talk you into believing different. Experts in weight control understand that simple calorie counting misses an important point (and bike riding, incidentally, burns off from about five hundred to eight hundred calories per hour, which is great in *anybody's* weight theory).

Quite often in weight problems, though, the body's appetite control has been disrupted. You eat more, you want to eat more, you eat more, your body demands more, you are "hungry" more, you eat more . . . you eat more . . . you eat more . . . etc. Did you really *need* that last bite? Well, perhaps so, or at least your body demanded it. You can either satisfy the demand or say no to your body and suffer.

But suppose your body hadn't demanded the last bite in the first place? Suppose your body had said, "No thanks, I'm already full and I don't need any more."

Wouldn't that be great?

That, in fact, is the secret to *permanent* weight control. A crash diet will surely take off pounds, just as a crash exercise or steam-bath program will take off pounds, but readjusting your metabolic balance by regular and continuous circulatory exercise will do the same job permanently. Adjusting your body's automatic appetite control, the "Apestat," means that you will eat as much as you *need,* not as much as your overweight body tells you it *wants.* But *not* all at once.

THE BEGINNER

Work up to full expert status gradually, in the following manner:

Let's assume you are a beginner with sedentary life and perhaps a pound or two more than you should be carrying. If you are not, if you qualify as perhaps an intermediate rider, then move on more quickly. Your body will tell you what level you are on, and when to move to a higher level.

And this is important enough to warn you that if the bicycle shop is more than about one mile from home, maybe you should just haul the bike home and work from there instead of trying to ride it home. You may have a few minor aches and pains getting accustomed to your new ten-speed, but these should not be the sprains of too much work too quickly or the strains of too much effort too soon.

The key word is *gradual.* Do everything gradually.

As a beginning rider you should confine your riding to distances of less than a mile for the first week or so, or until your legs tell you to stretch the distance a bit. Riding should be done on level ground, for the strain of hill riding on inexperienced legs can set you down for days, and cost you whatever you have gained.

While you are teaching your body this new way of moving, teach your hands how to shift smoothly and evenly, without wobbling. Shift up and down the gears frequently (though as you become more experienced, you will merely *select* your gear).

When you come to mild grades, which are good for you as a beginning rider with a week or so of experience, don't try to *muscle* over them. Either gear your way up, or walk up . . . unless you can get up a good bit of speed beforehand that will help carry you over. Muscling a bike up a hill is terribly fatiguing to both rider and bike, and discouraging when you find you aren't going to make it anyhow.

THE INTERMEDIATE RIDER

When you reach a physical level where you can cycle ten or fifteen miles over mildly varying terrain non-stop, say on a weekend jaunt around the area, and the level where you ride often enough to add up to a total of perhaps thirty miles every week (including the fifteen-mile jaunt), all of this riding without undue fatigue, you are an intermediate rider, and ready for more.

This is not a difficult plateau to reach, you will find. Miles add up quickly on a bike when you are having fun, and if you are really taking to this new sport, you will probably reach this level in but a few weeks. Ten miles per hour, for example, is not a breakneck speed on a bike, and yet at ten miles per hour one would only have to ride three hours per week to reach the thirty-mile, intermediate level. Of course all your riding will not be done at ten miles per hour, and some of it, as you continue to progress, will be done at higher speeds, so this is only a point maker and not a practical suggestion.

The intermediate rider should begin to think of his bicycle as a vehicle to get him to outings and day-long journeys. His bicycle is no longer a toy, but a useful device. And perhaps oddly, the intermediate rider begins to lavish more attention on his bike than when it was brand-new and shining from the store. He concerns himself with cleanliness and lubrication, and inspection and repair.

The intermediate rider's shorter bursts are from two to four or five miles daily without fatigue, and weekend jaunts of thirty miles non-stop without fatigue (though this does *not* mean without a pleasantly tired tingle to the legs).

THE EXPERT RIDER

When you reach the level where you ride perhaps fifty or so miles per week, with weekend trips as described before, and you do all of this regularly, without fatigue, you have become an expert bicycle rider. An expert really *rides* his bike.

People who are wrapped up in the sport of cycling do not find it at all unusual to put more than eighty miles per week on their bikes. They find speeds of twenty-five miles per hour comfortable and safe. They are the masters of their machines, and in their hands the modern well-constructed bicycle becomes what it is supposed to be, a superefficient, non-polluting vehicle that is healthful and enjoyable.

They can ride literally anywhere there is a road or lane or path, and many places where no path exists.

The expert uses his bike where others must dismount and push, because he has learned how to ride most efficiently. He uses his bike, loaded with gear, on tours for many days and nights on the road, and for camping. He competes with his bike against other experts in races and rallies, and over skill courses.

If you do not compete or camp with your bike and still wish to know that you are on the expert level, look at your riding. Can you ride fifty miles non-stop over average terrain with reasonably varying hills and dales, without undue fatigue? If so, you are an expert.

Do you ride (back and forth to work for example) an average of one hundred miles per week? You are an expert.

In all such riding, are you smooth and precise with steering and shifting, without a wobble or a poor shift? You are an expert. Through all of this, do you really love your bike and care for it as a friend (no need to get kinky about it, of course)? Through all of this, do you look forward to the ride? You are an expert.

There is no age limit, either way, for experts. It is in the riding, distance, and skill, and nothing else.

BUT YOU DON'T *have* TO BE AN EXPERT

The author of this, for whatever it might be worth, is not. Many, many riders who thoroughly enjoy their bikes and care for them as good pals are not in the above, "expert" class. So what? We just don't happen to ride that *far* every week, but we still ride. Dr. White, the distinguished cardiologist and presidential physician, who opened this chapter, is an addicted bicycle rider, and he once suggested that bike riding might even prevent peptic ulcers "provided we don't try to establish a new speed record every day."

So don't struggle to reach any certain "level" of riding, for that is foolish and health-defeating. Join us "intermediate experts" instead. Use and enjoy your bike and care for it, and you'll be at the very best level.

10

Maintenance Tips, Clubs, and Publications

MAINTENANCE

Deal at a reputable bike shop whenever you find that repairs beyond your depth have become necessary, and you should stay out of trouble. You have probably purchased your bike at such a shop in the first place and not at one of the usually cluttered and inefficient general stores such as Sears Roebuck (or any of the other all-purpose stores). While prices might be somewhat lower at these stores, the clerks are not specialists, bicycle information is difficult to obtain, repairs are nearly impossible to obtain, and the bicycles available are generally a motley collection of shopworn units with dangling parts.

Harsh, yes, but go check your own local department stores, then compare them with a shop that sells bikes, and services bikes, and loves bikes.

Then decide for yourself where you wish to purchase a bicycle, even if it does cost a dollar or two more.

There are ways to stay away from the service departments of bicycle establishments until really major service problems arise. And in the case of major companies (Schwinn is a good example), when you are forced to return you are protected, for they offer a *lifetime guarantee* on their bicycles.

In justice to stores like Sears, they could not afford to offer the same protection, for they didn't build the equipment in the first place, nor is it an item upon which they can concentrate their full attention. They are in a position where they must even charge their customers extra for *assembly* of the bicycle, unheard of at specialty bike shops. And while department stores are charging you to put the thing together, specialty stores are insisting that you take advantage of their *free* thirty-day tune-up to keep your bike in top condition.

If the frame breaks on a name-brand bike, the company will usually replace it. If the break is the result of normal use, the replacement will be free, parts and labor, forever. If a department-store frame breaks (after any standard guarantee period, of course) you must buy a new one.

If a brake pad wears out on a name brand, you return to the store where you bought it and pay a modest price for a new one. They know you . . . you are a customer who buys bicycles there. If a pad wears out on a department-store model, you must take the bike to the local repair shop, and they do not know you . . . but they *do* know that you buy your bicycles elsewhere. As a continuing, long-term customer, you are a doubtful commodity.

And in this bike boom, every bike store (specialty shop or department store) has taken on a new sophistication. They are "up" right now—they are flying, with business they can't possibly handle. But bike stores are always in the bicycle business. They'll still be in the same business when things have steadied down in a few years, and they keep this in mind. Try a department-store salesman who just sold the last model of the bike you wanted to buy. You need him, but *he* doesn't need *you*. He's *fat*. Maybe in a few years he'll need you, but not *now*, and he'll worry about that in a few years.

Follow the maintenance tips listed below and you should be able to avoid service shops while you digest all this talk of specialty shops versus department stores.

CLEANLINESS

Make bicycle cleanliness a regular habit. This need not be a drudging chore. Cleaning your bike can be fun if you concentrate on certain parts each day. Handlebar and fenders one day, brakes the next, wheels another day, on schedule, with each day's work taking but a moment or two. Your bike will never get really dirty with this method of cleaning, and the cleaning doesn't get to be a hated job.

ADJUST EVERY MONTH

Side play in front and rear brake levers.
Brake blocks and pads to wheel rim.
Chain.

LUBRICATE EVERY MONTH
(or more frequently with heavy use)

All levers (oil).
Head races and crown race (grease).
Brake joints (oil).
Wheel hub, front and rear (oil).
Coaster brake (oil).
Chain (oil or chain lube—remove and soak in cleaner, then oil, every three months, *more frequently in poor weather or in sandy or dirty areas*).
Bottom bracket bearings (grease).
Pedals (grease).

ADJUST AND LUBRICATE WHEN REQUIRED

Reflectors and headlights.
Tire pressure.
Headset bearings (grease).
Wheel alignment.
Handlebar (at least two and a half inches of stem must be in headset; the same is true for seat post in seat tube).

Oil the chain at the front of the front sprocket while turning the pedal backward.

Front and rear hub cones (oil).

Pedal cone and bearings (grease).

Front and rear dérailleur mechanisms and cables (oil).

Three-speed hub indicator (be sure knurled lock nut is secure after adjustment).

GENERAL MAINTENANCE

Polish enamel surfaces with any good liquid wax, and use touch-up paint where needed.

Chrome-plated parts should be kept waxed or coated with an oil film in extreme wet conditions and when in storage.

White-sidewall tires can be cleaned easily with scouring pads.

Leather saddles are stiff when new. You can soften the leather before riding by gently beating on it with a pipe or hammer. Neat's-foot oil can also be used to soften leather, but any dyes might come off on clothing in using this process.

BICYCLE CLUBS

For further information on bicycles and cycling activities, contact the following clubs:

Touring

American Youth Hostels
20 West Seventeenth Street
New York, N.Y. 10011
For low cost accommodations while touring on bicycles.

Bicycle Touring League of America
260 West Twenty-sixth Street
New York, N.Y. 10001
For bicycle touring information.

International Bicycle Touring Society
846 Prospect Street
La Jolla, California 92037
Providing information on bicycle trips in the United States and abroad.

League of American Wheelmen
5118 West Foster Avenue
Chicago, Illinois 60630
This is the national organization of recreational bicyclists.

Bicycle Institute of America
122 East Forty-second Street
New York, N.Y. 10017
For information on establishing bikeways in your community and other bicycle information and literature.

Bicycle Racing

Amateur Bicycle League of America
Box 669, Wall St. Station
New York, N.Y. 10005
The governing body of competitive bicycling in the United States

Eastern Cycling Federation
42-33–205th Street
Bayside, New York 11361
For East Coast bicycle enthusiasts.

Eastern Intercollegiate Cycling Association
95 East Deshler Avenue
Columbus, Ohio 43206
A division of Amateur Bicycle League of America governing college-level bicycle racing.

Canadian Wheelmen's Association
4000 Beaubien Street East
Montreal, Quebec, Canada
For Canadian cycling enthusiasts.

MANUFACTURERS WILLING TO HELP

For catalogues and cycling information, write to the Cycling Activities Department of each of these bike makers.

Schwinn Bicycle Company
1856 North Kostner Avenue
Chicago, Illinois 60639

The Huffman Manufacturing Company
P. O. Box 1204
Dayton, Ohio 45401

PARTS CATALOGUES

The Complete Handbook of Cycling
Big Wheel, Ltd.
310 Holly street
Denver, Colorado 80220

The Handbook of Cycl-ology
Wheel Goods Corporation
2737 Hennepin Avenue
Minneapolis, Minnesota 55408
($2)

PUBLICATIONS

The Complete Book of Bicycling
by Eugene A. Sloane
Trident Press ($9.95)

Dérailleur Lightweights
A New Dimension in Cycling
by A. Fred DeLong
Schwinn Bicycle Company (free)

Cycling
by Roy Ald
Grosset & Dunlap ($1)

Bicycle Riding Clubs, Bike Racing on Campus, Bike Regulations in the Community, Bike Fun, Bicycle Safety Set, Bikeways.
Bicycle Institute of America
(see BICYCLE CLUBS)

Anybody's Bike Book
by Tom Cuthbertson
Ten Speed Press
2510 Bancroft Way
Berkeley, California 94704
($3)

Bicycling! Magazine
256 Sutter Street
San Francisco, California 94108
(Monthly, $6 per year)

American Cycling
American Cycling Press
1470 Fernwood Drive
Oakland, California 94611
(10 issues per year, $3 per year)

CYCLING FILMS

The Road to Adventure, Tour of Kettering, The Corona London-Holyhead Cycle Race, 1962, A Race Apart.
The Huffy Film Library
Box 1036
Dayton, Ohio 45401

Magic of the Bicycle
Schwinn Bicycle Company
1856 North Kostner Avenue
Chicago, Illinois 60639

Index